The
Canary
Islander

Barrie Mahoney worked as a teacher and head teacher in the south west of England, and then became a school inspector in England and Wales. A new life and career as a newspaper reporter in Spain's Costa Blanca led to him launching and editing an English language newspaper in the Canary Islands. Following the successful publication of his novels, 'Journeys and Jigsaws' and 'Threads and Threats', and then 'Letters from the Atlantic', 'Living the Dream', 'Expat Survival', 'Message in a Bottle' and 'Twitters from the Atlantic' that give an amusing and reflective view of life abroad, he enjoys life in the sun. Barrie writes regular columns for newspapers and magazines in Spain, Portugal, Ireland, Australia, South Africa, Canada, UK and the USA. He also designs mobile apps and websites to promote the Canary Islands and expat life, and is often asked to contribute to radio programmes about expat life.

Visit the author's websites:

www.barriemahoney.com
www.thecanaryislander.com

Other books by Barrie Mahoney

Journeys and Jigsaws (Vanguard Press) 2009 ISBN: 978 184386 538 4 (Paperback and Kindle)

Threads and Threats (Vanguard Press) 2011 ISBN: 978 184386 646 6 (Paperback and Kindle)

Letters from the Atlantic (Vanguard Press) 2011 ISBN: 978 184386 645 9 (Paperback and Kindle)

Living the Dream (The Canary Islander Publishing) 2011
ISBN: 978 145076 704 0 (Paperback, Kindle and iBook)

Expat Survival (The Canary Islander Publishing) 2012
ISBN: 978-1479130481 (Paperback, Kindle and iBook)

Message in a Bottle (The Canary Islander Publishing) 2012
ISBN: 978-1480031005 (Paperback, Kindle and iBook)

Twitters from the Atlantic (The Canary Islander Publishing) 2012
ISBN: 978-1480033986 (Paperback, Kindle and iBook)

Other publications by Barrie Mahoney

News from the Canary Islands (Kindle) 2011

Twitters from the Atlantic (Kindle) 2011

Apps for iPhone, iPad, iTouch and Android devices
Download from iTunes and Google Play stores

CanaryIsle

ExpatInfo

CanaryGay

ESCAPE TO THE SUN

BARRIE MAHONEY

The Canary Islander Publishing

The
Canary
Islander

ISBN 978-0957544444
www.barriemahoney.com

First Published in 2013
The Canary Islander Publishing

The
Canary
Islander

DEDICATION

This book is dedicated to expats all over the world who dream of a new life, new experiences, new cultures, new opportunities to experience, taste and smell the excitement of a place that is of their own choosing and not merely based upon an accident of birth.

The
Canary
Islander

Acknowledgements

I would like to thank all those people that I have met on my journey to where I am now.

To supportive friends who helped me to overcome the many problems and frustrations that I faced and taught me much about learning to adapt to a new culture. Also, to friends in the UK, or scattered around the world, who have kept in touch despite being so far away.

To the people that I met whilst working as a newspaper reporter and editor in Spain and the Canary Islands, and for the privilege of sharing their successes and challenges in life.

To my life partner, David, for his constant love and support and for travelling the journey together.

Disclaimer

This is a book about real people, real places and real events, but names of people and companies have been changed to avoid any embarrassment.

The
Canary
Islander

Preface

'Escape to the Sun'

'Escape to the Sun' was written during a year of relative turmoil in the Canary Islands and Spain, as well as across Europe in general. Increased concerns about very high unemployment levels, the increasing impact of the banking crisis upon ordinary people, bankruptcies and home repossessions have all led to increasing uncertainty in both the local and expat population of the islands.

The political situation has not been good either, with political uncertainties, scandals and 'in-fighting' within the ruling Partido Popular (Conservative) party, affecting the popularity and possible tenure of the Spanish Prime Minister. Even the once highly popular Spanish Royal family has come in for considerable criticism for unwise financial dealings from the usually respectful Spanish media.

As I write this, the old chestnut surrounding the status of Gibraltar has raised its ugly head once again. Most observers agree that this is a regular ploy by both the Spanish and UK Governments during periods of internal discontent and unrest to focus the attention of the media and general population upon issues other than the economy, unemployment and unpopularity of the government. However, such issues are unsettling for both businesses and expats alike, and can cause needless concern and anxiety for all.

Building sites that were once identified as areas for smart new development for expat homes, shopping centres and offices remain silent, sale boards of both completed, as well as incomplete, properties abound. Many Spanish people have left the country for work elsewhere in Europe and beyond. In most towns and cities, there is an abundance of empty shops, bars, offices and homes, and the once lively Costas are no longer the bustling areas that they once were.

Looking back, it should not have come as such a surprise. Spain's economy, as well as that in many other countries, grew far too quickly to sustain, and the people behind the system grew both greedy and complacent. The bubble had to burst eventually, together with its disastrous consequences.

During the early days of the European banking crisis, it was a popular sport for British economic commentators to forecast the imminent collapse of the euro, the European banking system, as well as the European project in general. Thankfully, none of these predictions have come true; they may in the future, but I doubt it. However, more recently, the British media has turned the spotlight upon the fragile state of the British economy, which is not as strong as first thought. Suddenly, attention has shifted away from the failures of Spain, Portugal, Greece, Ireland and Italy to the many deficiencies within the UK itself.

The unpopular truth for commentators is that, despite support from the European Union, Spain is nowhere near a lost cause. In the last two years, Spanish manufacturers that traditionally focused upon the home market have turned their attention to the global market. As a result, exports have reached a record high. Even the most jingoistic of commentators are beginning to realise that Spain has the capacity, ability and wherewithal to rectify its economic problems, and is not another Greece or Portugal as was popular opinion a short time ago.

The European Union is not a popular concept in the UK. I doubt it ever will be, and there is a possibility that the UK may leave it in the future, or be part of some other formation that will accommodate its unique and distorted perspective of the continent, and ease it finally and painfully away from the days of Empire to a modern state working within and being a true part of a united Europe. However, as it currently stands, the EU has been a true blessing, for it has provided the opportunity for anyone to live and work in any other EU country, without visas and work permits, which was unimaginable forty years ago.

So where does this leave the expat in Europe? Well, it is true that there is now greater uncertainty about the future than I have known for many years. However, I am and always have been an optimist and I have little time for the cynical "my glass is half empty" brigade that appears to be the most damaging part of the UK's current psyche.

People will always have dreams and passions, for that is the true essence of the human condition. For some, this may mean a larger home, a new car, or climbing a mountain. For many others, like myself, it is the dream of a new life, new experiences, new cultures, the opportunity to experience, taste and smell the excitement in a place that is of our own choosing and not merely based upon an accident of birth.

For many, the dreams will be of a less stressful life, an opportunity to be challenged by new experiences, new and exciting work opportunities, a place where there is a high quality of life in which a young family may grow. For others, it may be the dream of a carefree, long, happy and healthy retirement, but for all it is an 'Escape to the Sun'.

Eating, Drinking and Health

The
Canary
Islander

The Mango Tree

We have a fine mango tree in our garden. As yet, it is a little on the small side to bear fruit, but it looks very healthy. The tree has a thick trunk and lush green leaves, and so we live in hope that one day it will produce fruit for our breakfast. Meanwhile, I have to content myself with fresh mango from a local farmer who has discovered that both mango and papaya fruits make a useful addition to his income.

Before I moved to the Canary Islands, I don't recall ever eating mango, other than from a tin or in one of those over-rated and often overpriced smoothies that became so fashionable a few years ago. However, since arriving in Gran Canaria, mango has formed part of my breakfast fruit salad. Their gleaming reddish purple skins scream 'Good Morning' when they are looked at and the melt-in-the-mouth flesh, sensual sweetness and rich citrus aroma, together with local bananas and pineapple, washed down with papaya juice, make for a healthy and heady start to a new day, as well as being a rich source of vitamin C.

Mangoes arrived in the Canary Islands, and parts of coastal Spain, from Spain's Empire in the tropics during the 18th century, with the first mangoes being brought from the Philippines on galleons. The fruit originates from India and the days when the mango tree was used as an exotic and ornamental presence gracing the gardens of wealthy Canarians has now developed into a lucrative crop for some Canarian farmers who grow the fruit all year round in greenhouses, as well as open-air plantations.

Mangoes contain more sugar than most other fruit, because they are harvested as soon as they ripen on the plant. Canarian and Spanish mangoes are also the only ones, I am told, that reach European markets in their own protective wax jackets; unlike competing fruit from other parts of the world that are treated with fungicides and edible varnish. The fruit is picked individually, positioned upside down on the ground for about an hour and a half to release the sap that would otherwise stain its beautiful, velvety skin. Then the fruit is packed into crates and transported to its destination. Most of the Canary Islands' crop is exported to Peninsular Spain, the UK, Germany and France.

The fruit is a versatile and important part of many recipes with fruit smoothies, ice creams, juices and milkshakes being popular uses for the fruit. However, for those who know their mangoes, they can be served as pickles, spicy mustards, chutneys or simply served as a side dish and eaten raw with salt, soy sauce, or chilli, which are some of the more unusual serving suggestions.

Nothing is ever perfect, not even this fruit, and so a brief warning to those who are susceptible to contact dermatitis. Mango peel and sap, as well as mango leaves and stems contain uroshiol, a chemical that is present in poison ivy and may cause an allergic reaction for some people.

As well as being a delicious fruit, the tourist industry is now waking up to the idea that as the fruit is grown in often stunningly beautiful surroundings close to the sea, dishes that include mango, as well as other locally grown exotic fruit, are adding a new dimension to local tourism on the islands. Mangoes can be served as a seasonal, local fresh fruit or included in a whole variety of both savoury, as well as sweet dishes, which leaves a lasting positive impression upon the islands' visitors.

I have just checked our mango tree yet again; still, no fruit. However, I do believe that maybe next year will be our first mango harvest! I live in hope.

Lady Balfour to the rescue

I like pasta and rice, but for me nothing quite beats the humble potato. I don't mind whether potatoes are boiled, mashed, fried, baked or sautéed, although, in my opinion, nothing quite beats the good old British chip (not those ghastly French Fries!) or a jacket potato filled with baked beans and cheese. Maybe my love of the humble potato, a much under-rated vegetable in Spain, comes from my Irish ancestry, and that country's strong dependency upon a successful potato crop in years gone by. Indeed, it was the potato famine that led my great grandfather from Ireland to England, but that is a different story.

Living in Gran Canaria, I quickly discovered the delights of a simple delicacy, 'papas con mojo', which is readily available in most tapas bars and restaurants on the island. This is a dish of small, new Canarian potatoes, boiled in sea salt, and served with a delicious, spicy, 'mojo' sauce, and preferably freshly prepared and not bottled. If you haven't tried this dish already, then you really should when you next visit.

For the past few years, I have been shocked to find that whenever I try to buy a sack of large potatoes for baking from my local supermarket, they are not from the Canary Islands, or even Spain. Instead they are imported from the UK, from Lincolnshire, just a short distance from where I spent my childhood. These tasteless, soggy objects marketed as potatoes are actually very cheap to buy, and I suspect that there is very little profit in them for anyone in the supply chain. Now, I am not about to deny the good farmers of Lincolnshire a decent income from their potato exports, but I would much prefer to buy the more flavoursome varieties that are grown in the Canary Islands, or Spain.

This situation is about to change with the local Spar supermarket food chain giving 14,000 kilos of organic seed potato to fifteen island farmers. The company aims to market 150,000 and 200,000 kilos of potatoes in Spar stores within four months, in an attempt to raise local production, thereby avoiding the necessity to import potatoes from abroad. Currently, island grown potatoes meets only 5 per cent of local demand, with 90 per cent being imported from overseas.

It is the Lady Balfour variety of Scottish seed potato that has been imported from Scotland, and Spar has undertaken to cover the costs of production, without affecting the market price for farmers. In addition, the scheme will test how the seed potato develops in different municipalities on the island, depending on the weather and terrain, together with an evaluation of the profitability of each plot used.

As a bonus, it is anticipated that the Spar scheme will help to maintain fifty jobs and create a further 60 new opportunities for unemployed people. It is also hoped that similar schemes will be established to encourage onion and garlic production as well. It is imaginative schemes such as this, as well as a change in the attitude of some companies to one of 'giving something back to the community' that will help to ease the unemployment crisis on the islands, and give renewed hope to local growers, as well as the unemployed.

By the way, I guess you are wondering who was Lady Balfour? Well, she was an English farmer, and an organic farming pioneer and the first women to study farming in a British university. She wrote 'The Living Soil', which was a popular book written to encourage farmers to follow organic production methods, and may be regarded as one of the world's true organic farming pioneers. I bet Lady Balfour recognised a decent chip when she saw one!

The Banana Fights Back

I was pleased to read a recent news article commenting that Asda is the first UK supermarket to sell Canarian bananas through 230 of its UK stores. This initiative represents the first time in recent history that bananas from the Canary Islands are sold commercially outside the usual markets in Spain and Portugal. Other UK supermarkets, including Marks and Spencer, are also reportedly examining a similar scheme.

Until recently, I had not been aware that the carbon footprint of the banana, as well as other tropical fruit and vegetables, is very high. As well as Canary Islands bananas being a better quality and more flavoursome variety, Asda is also aiming to reduce the banana's carbon footprint, and will therefore cancel its Central American imports in favour of bananas from the Canary Islands. Conveniently, importing a better banana to the UK also comes with added benefits, making good commercial, as well as environmental sense.

In future, Canarian bananas destined for Asda stores will be shipped to Peninsular Spain and then transported by road to ripening centres in the UK. This will mean that the journey will take just four days compared with twenty-four days for produce from Central America, which is a reduction in transportation time of over 80 per cent. As a result, the fruit will be much fresher by the time that it reaches British stores. Canarian bananas will be sold under the well known Fyffes brand in the UK.

It is appropriate that the UK throws its full weight behind the Canarian banana. After all, it was in the 19th Century that an Englishman living in the Canary Islands spotted a business opportunity from bananas. His company imported the dwarf banana from the Far East and grew it on the islands. The company exported the bananas to England, and by 1878 many cargoes of bananas were leaving the Canary Islands for the UK.

Few people nowadays realise the impact that bananas from the Canary Islands made to the economy of the UK. Bananas were once unloaded in the very centre of what is now London's vibrant financial district, which takes its name from the No. 10 Warehouse of the South Quay Import Dock, built in 1952 for the Canary Islands' fruit trade. This grey glass, concrete and steel paradise proudly retains the name Canary Wharf to this day.

As holiday makers to the Canary Islands will already know, it is the warm sea currents that give the Canary islands a sub tropical climate. Despite the popularity of the islands as an all year round tourist destination, it is the banana that is still the islands' most important product after tourism. Away from the sun-drenched beaches, extensive banana plantations dominate the landscape of the archipelago. The varieties currently grown in the Canary Islands are dwarf bananas, which are smaller, creamier, sweeter, and have a more intense flavour than the varieties produced in Latin America and the Caribbean.

Personally, I much prefer the Canary Islands banana to any of the other tasteless varieties, but then I guess I am biased. Do try a real Canary Islands' banana for yourself and you will see what I mean. Incidentally, local banana flavoured rum is also delicious, as well as being made from local bananas!

Cockroaches in the Clinic

I met a visitor to the island in a very distressed state last week. Paul and his wife had been visiting the island for many years and, although his wife was not blessed with the best of health, they had always found Gran Canaria to be a relaxing and health promoting place to visit. That was until a few days ago when the nightmare began.

Paul's wife, Anne, suffered from a collapsed lung and the couple immediately sought medical treatment. Anne was taken by ambulance to a hospital recommended by the tour company. Upon arrival at the hospital, Paul had to pay the private ambulance 300 euros before they would release his wife from the vehicle and take her into the building for urgent medical care.

The ambulance was a private one, and not one provided by the Health Service, and the ambulance drivers had decided to take Anne and Paul to a private clinic, instead of the NHS hospital that Paul and the tour company representative had asked for. Paul soon realised this and tried to make his wishes clear to the ambulance staff, but they refused. As Anne was in great distress, Paul realised that he had no option other than to accept the option of the private clinic, which Paul assumed would be covered under the European Health Card system (previously E111), or his travel insurance policy.

Upon entry to the private clinic, Paul was immediately asked for his credit card, which was duly debited with the sum of 1500 euros. Although the couple had medical insurance, they were told that they would have to "pay now and claim back later" as the cost of Anne's consultation and tests would have to be paid for in advance, and the clinic did not have a direct payment agreement with the insurance company.

Although Paul was reasonably happy with the consultation and tests that were carried out, he was less than happy with the hygiene within the clinic. He spotted several cockroaches in the waiting area, and was appalled when one appeared in the treatment room, which the doctor duly stamped on, before recommencing Anne's tests and emergency treatment.

Eventually, Paul was told that Anne would have to be transferred to a larger hospital, which would have more advanced facilities to deal with Anne's condition. An ambulance was called, for which Paul had to pay another 300 euros, and Anne was taken to an excellent, and well resourced Health Service hospital, which Anne should have been taken to in the first place, and where she would have received emergency treatment free of charge under the reciprocal European health scheme. As Paul was waiting anxiously to hear news of his wife, he revealed the stress that he had been under during the previous few hours.

Paul's credit cards and bank account had been decimated, and it was unlikely that the couple would be able to return home for a week or two, as Anne would not be able travel. Instead, the couple would have to rent an apartment, as they were due out of their holiday hotel the following day. Paul was in the process of phoning relatives and asking them to send funds urgently to him.

What should have been a relaxing holiday had turned into a nightmare for the couple, and they were exasperated by the confusion created by obtaining appropriate medical care. It was clear that both private clinics and the private ambulance were taking advantage of a vulnerable couple in great distress. This, together with a lack of awareness of what to do in an emergency, a lack of awareness of the terms of their travel insurance policy, as well as the scope of the European Health Card system exaggerated a serious problem, which others were happy to greedily exploit. This is a situation that is by no means unique to the Canary Islands, and I am aware of similar cases in other popular tourist destinations.

Finally, as much as I admire the tenacity of cockroaches, as well as being aware that their species may well outlive the human race, clearly their place is not inside a medical clinic. Due to the greed of some private health care operators, I suspect that the island may have lost two tourists who have for many years regarded the island as a welcoming and relaxing destination.

Health care - are you really covered?

As I was growing up, my Mum always warned me never to talk about politics, sex or religion at the dinner table. For me, she also added later that I should not talk about vegetarianism or blood sports, as I tended to upset some of our more carnivorous family members and friends with my strongly held views. I usually followed her advice at the dinner table, but with 'Twitters', I sense a new feeling of liberation.

Maybe Margaret Thatcher, as well as the National Health Service, should also be added to the list of 'no-nos' in order to avoid unnecessary conflict. Both these areas provoke intense discussion, and I have yet to meet someone who does not have a strong opinion of the former, although maybe less are concerned about the latter - that is, until something goes wrong.

Both my parents worked for the UK's National Health Service; they were proud of it and the part that they played in it during the early years of its establishment in the UK. However, I was always warned by my father to avoid hospital and medical treatment at all costs, and unless it was a matter of life and death. I grew up with the view that private health care was like a parasite on the back of the NHS, and that medical care should be needs based, and not led by an ability to pay. Later, my father would have been horrified to learn that I had, and still have, a private medical health policy, albeit one issued at a very favourable rate by a friendly society when I was an 18-year-old civil servant, and which I still have to this day. I also now have to admit that I have been very grateful for it and the protection that it has given to both my partner and myself.

I first made use of private health care many years ago when my partner became very ill. It was at the time when there was only one MRI scanner covering the whole area where we lived, and this portable unit was trundled around to six hospitals in a large van once each week. The consultant told us that we would have to wait around six months before we could get an appointment for an MRI scan. Sensing our concern, we were asked if we had private medical insurance. I nodded reluctantly and the immediate response was, "Will next Thursday morning be convenient?" I agreed, felt guilty, a traitor to the cause, but also very relieved.

So what does all this have to do with expat life? Well, when we moved to Spain, it was quite common for those under retirement age to rely on the Spanish Health Service, as well as choosing to return to the UK for certain health treatments. This they did by using form E111 and claiming that they were visitors, even though they were permanent residents, and questions were rarely asked. Form E111 was intended to facilitate free and reciprocal health care, in cases of emergency, for visitors to member EU countries. I recall one neighbour proudly telling me that he returned to the UK every six months specifically to get new E111 forms for himself and his extended family, and this is how his entire family had been cared for in his ten years of permanent residence in

Spain. Several months of misuse later, our neighbour became very angry when his local doctor quite rightly refused to treat his mother-in-law, and said that the family were not entitled to free health care in Spain, and as they were under retirement age they should seek private medical care instead.

Of course, more recently, and mostly due to the world recession, the reciprocal health care systems in Spain and other European countries have been tightened up considerably. However, it can lead to situations where expats believe that they are covered under the local health service. This may be because they are working, are retired or have a health card to cover their self-employment. However, at a time of crisis, many discover that they are not covered.

Do check that you are covered for free health care in the country where you live, or that you have a private medical insurance in place.

Care for Elderly Expats

In their haste to move to the sun, many expats ignore the facts relating to getting old and the possibility of becoming infirm. There are now several generations of expats, who found themselves in a good financial position following the rapid rise in UK houses prices a decade or so ago, and others who managed to retire early on good pensions. Added to this were the advantages of exchange rates, which worked heavily in favour of British expats, meaning that those fortunate enough to be receiving an early pension, or in receipt of a private income, could maintain a much better standard of living in Spain and France than in the UK.

If we are fortunate, we get old, and for some expats this means returning to their countries of origin where perhaps they have maintained a second home, could be cared for by relatives or return to the UK care system and take advantage of retirement, care homes and sheltered accommodation. Other expats prefer to remain in their chosen country, taking advantage of the warm climate, which for many has eased conditions, such as arthritis, rheumatism and other age related conditions. However, the problems begin once one partner dies, or health issues become serious. What happens next for an elderly or infirm expat living in Spain?

It is still the custom and tradition for many Spanish families to look after their own. In many ways, this is one of the favourable characteristics of Spanish people and their culture. Generalisation is always dangerous, but traditionally the Spanish see it as their duty to look after the elderly and sick members of their families. It is still often the case that upon marriage, the young couple will continue to live in the family home, maybe in an apartment converted from a garage or in a newly built extension. As the family grows, grandparents tend to help to look after their grandchildren. Later in life, it is the young couple, now middle aged, who move into the main dwelling, with the elderly folk moving into the converted apartment built originally for the youngsters. It is a tradition that usually works well, and although this model of care is rapidly changing, particularly in Spanish cities and due to the pressures of modern living, it is still the pattern of life in rural Spain and in the Canary Islands.

As a result of care being provided by the family, unlike in the UK, residential homes for the elderly are largely unnecessary and unavailable. There are very few in the Canary Islands, and the ones that do exist are mostly run by religious orders of nuns, and cater mainly for the local Canarian population and not for elderly expats.

As a newspaper reporter in the Costa Blanca, I remember visiting a new privately built and operated residential home, designed and marketed specifically for the expat population. It offered a high standard of care in several languages. A clever entrepreneur had spotted a market opportunity, which came as a great relief to many of the resident expats that I interviewed at the time. However, such a development was unique in the area at the time and I was aware of a long waiting list for a place.

I am unaware of similar accommodation for the elderly expat being available in the Canary Islands; for example, most care is provided through the islands' social services, which is now greatly reduced due to budgetary reductions. Other care is provided privately in homes through a variety of carers, registered or otherwise. Sadly, such services are often transitory, and not available on a long-term basis, which is important if the elderly expat comes to rely upon such services in their home. Overall, it is not a good position, and I suspect that this issue will become more serious as the expat population in many countries becomes older and more frail.

If any readers have more information about residential homes for the elderly in their areas, which are specific to the expat population, do please let me know. I will post any useful information on the Expat Survival section of my website.

Wildlife and Weather

The
Canary
Islander

Remember, Remember - the Fifth of November

Since moving to Spain and the Canary Islands, I have always thought it a little inappropriate and insensitive that, when living in a Catholic country, some British expats still celebrate Bonfire Night. The execution of Catholic, Guy Fawkes, in 1606 for trying to blow up the British Houses of Parliament, is still celebrated and remembered by burning an effigy of the poor man on a flaming bonfire. Still, I guess it takes all sorts in an expat world.

There was a time that I enjoyed fireworks; however, not any more. Since first having a dog, a corgi called Ollie in the UK, I have come to dread this annual orgy of explosive excess. Ollie hated fireworks, and from the time that the first banger was lit, he would tremble and shake; he quickly became more uncontrollable as the evening progressed and was clearly in great distress. He would run away, anywhere around the house, to find a safe place, all to no avail. What made matters even worse was that whatever we did to try and help, nothing seemed to work. Eventually, Ollie would collapse with exhaustion; it was pitiful to see.

We hoped that Ollie would grow out of this annual distress, but he didn't. Eventually, we took him to the vet, who prescribed tranquillisers, which we administered just before the fateful night. This too was a great mistake and it was even worse to see Ollie, still in great distress, but now staggering around the house, with legs like jelly, unable to escape to anywhere that he perceived as a safe space. Fortunately, after Bonfire Night, it was usually over and done with for another year, but with maybe another short burst of activity on New Year's Eve.

Now, living in the Canary Islands with Bella our dog, and Mac our cat, the problem is potentially much worse. Despite the recession, it seems that many of our neighbours still have plenty of money to burn, which they do to great excess from a day or two before Halloween until just after 6 January. Halloween, Bonfire Night, Christmas, New Year, as well as King's Day are all great excuses to let off as many fireworks as possible. In addition, birthdays, anniversaries or maybe a new job and the many fiestas are all great excuses for a party; complete with fireworks, and the noisier the better.

It is pitiful to hear the dogs barking, of which there are many in our area, and often in terror, with each explosion. No self-respecting cat is to be seen anywhere and, I guess, that most have the good sense to hide themselves away for the evening.

Bella spends her evening inside our living room with us, barking and shaking. Doors and windows are closed, shutters firmly closed with either the television switched on or music playing loudly. In some cases, I know that aromatherapy using lavender oil also helps. I have also heard that it is possible to buy CDs of special music, especially for pets trying to cope in these circumstances. I have not tried these, but it may well be worth finding a copy.

As for Mac the cat, is he bothered? Not in the slightest. He looks at Bella with distain, yawns, and falls asleep on his favourite rug.

Float like a Butterfly, Sting like a Bee

As a child growing up in fenland Lincolnshire, I always seemed to be attacked by wasps, yet only once by a bumblebee, which had the misfortune to be squashed, as I was performing a dramatic handstand on our lawn. I also well remember one of my parents' friends dying from the effects of a wasp sting, which to an impressionable child didn't exactly endear me to any insect with a sting.

As I grew older, I began to develop a greater respect for bees, as opposed to wasps. I learned that bees very rarely attack unless provoked. However, my hatred of wasps continued to be fuelled as I grew older by the sight of my partner frantically trying to escape a swarm of angry wasps that had been disturbed by his enthusiastic attempts to trim our fast growing hedge with an electric hedge trimmer. Those wasps were certainly angry and expressed their displeasure upon my partner with a vengeance; I have never seen him move so quickly as he did that morning.

Since living in Spain's Costa Blanca and the Canary Islands, I have never seen a wasp. I began to believe the myth that there are none of these evil insects on the Islands. However, I now understand that I am incorrect in this assumption and, to the contrary, wasps have been singled out as a major threat to native butterfly populations on the Canary Islands. Although reportedly only living in the Western

Islands, due to higher humidity levels, wasps are now spreading to the whole archipelago.

As for the humble bee, I had not seen any in our garden until recently when, thanks to a huge and beautiful lavender plant that a friend gave us, is now home to many bees. Yes, I have learned to keep away from them, but also learned to be grateful to the honey bees on these Islands, and for the beautiful Canary Islands' honey that they produce, as well as their generous contribution to the much loved honey rum, also produced on the island. Local honey certainly has a special and unique flavour, unlike any of the supermarket offerings that I have previously bought in the UK.

I have also learned that the Canary Islands bee is unique to these Islands. The UK bee is striped yellow and black, with a white tip on the abdomen, whereas bees living in the Canary Islands have no yellow bands, and they are just plain old black and white. For an island that is rich in colour, culture and diversity, this is something of an anomaly!

As for wasps, the Government in the Canary Islands is trying hard to control the damage that these insects cause to the beehives on the islands, and is working with beekeepers to locate and restrict the damage that they cause.

As a child, I often used to ask what was the point of wasps? Apart from being given the unconvincing answer of how important they were in clearing away rotting fruit. I remained cynical about their purpose in the greater scheme of things. However, I have recently discovered that a particular species of wasp living in the Canary Islands, commonly known as the Ensign wasp, is actually rather useful. This wasp, which looks a bit like a black spider is relatively harmless to humans, but is a parasite of cockroaches. The females of the species lay their eggs inside the egg cases of cockroaches and the wasp larvae eat the cockroach eggs.

I know that many readers of my 'Twitters' are not too keen on my cockroach stories, but this Twitter does have a happy ending. So, if you happen to see an Ensign wasp in the Canary Islands, just welcome it with open arms!

Animal Welfare in Spain and the Canary Islands

I have very little to complain about my life in Spain and the Canary Islands. It is a wonderful place to live and work, and the decision to leave the UK for a new life in the sun was the right one for us. However, I am sometimes asked if there is anything that I regret and, apart from leaving family and friends behind, I would say that animal welfare is my main concern.

Over the years, animal cruelty in Spain and the Canary Islands has horrified and distressed me. I long for the equivalent of the UK's RSPCA, which, although not perfect, does its best to fight and challenge cruelty in the UK, with the full backing of law. In Spain, this responsibility is mostly left to the police. In recent years there have been signs that this responsibility is beginning to be taken seriously, but frankly I have little confidence in a police force that used stray cats and dogs for target practice on the deserted beaches of the Costa Blanca early in the morning, which was reported to me by a correspondent some years ago. Fortunately, such horrific incidents were stopped by the local Town Hall, because of its detrimental effect upon tourism.

Similarly, the poisoning of stray cats, which are treated as vermin, is relatively common in the Canary Islands. Again, this was stopped by Town Halls in the tourist areas of the south, as it was not viewed as acceptable by tourists staying in nearby hotels, many of whom witnessed the carnage. Sadly, this barbaric practice still continues in local villages and I remember the desperate cries of a child in the village where I live, whose much-loved cat was in its final death throes as a result of such barbaric activities.

The global recession has made matters much worse, with many pets being abandoned at the beginning of the summer holidays, because families claim that they cannot afford boarding or veterinary fees when they go away on holiday. The numbers of healthy abandoned animals who are destroyed in Spain and the Canary Islands remain at horrific levels, yet pet shops remain full of puppies and kittens for sale, many imported from puppy and kitten farms and transported over long distances from Eastern Europe.

Fortunately, animal welfare has improved over the years, thanks mainly to the large expat population in Spain. There are many groups of Scandinavian, German and British expats working closely with their Spanish and Canarian neighbours to rehome stray and abandoned animals. In the Canary Islands, for instance, large numbers of dogs are flown to Germany and the Netherlands for rehoming each year by groups of dedicated volunteers.

During my time as a reporter in the Costa Blanca, I began to ask many questions about why there were so many healthy looking, but stray dogs in municipal pounds. The answer gradually became clearer when I moved to the Canary Islands. Much is due to cultural traditions. Many people on the islands have dogs and cats as pets, and they are mostly well cared for, but not in the traditional British sense. In the Canary

Islands, many dogs are let out of their homes onto the streets after breakfast to roam freely until the end of the day when they return home for their food. In the old days this may have been acceptable in villages without cars, but nowadays it is both foolish and dangerous, yet the tradition persists. I have known of many instances where a well-meaning expat has seen a dog roaming the streets and, thinking it must be homeless, has taken it to the municipal pound for rehoming or worse. The reality is that in many cases Pedro has been let out for the day, has a home, and intended to return to it for his evening meal, until the well-meaning expat intervened.

The spaying and neutering of cats and dogs is not the norm in Spain and the Canary Islands, as it is in the UK and many other European countries. This is mainly because it is very expensive, and there are few opportunities for this service to be provided free of charge to less advantaged families, thereby reducing the stray dog and cat population.

Life in Spain and the Canary Islands is pretty good overall, with the exception of animal welfare. The old adage that you can judge a civilised society by the way that it treats its animals is very true, and the country's leaders and its citizens would do well to remember it.

Through the Rainbow

We have had some heavy rain in the Canary Islands recently. It is not typical to have this quantity of rain during November, as it is usually reserved for a few gloomy days in February. Still, as we are all now becoming aware, weather patterns are changing across the World. In the mostly warm and arid climate of the south of the island where I live, a little rain is welcome, but even rain lovers had a shock last week.

It was indeed a heavy storm and, once again, rain had found its way through two doors of our home. It is not usual for thresholds to be fitted to the bottom of doors, as is usually the case in the UK and other Northern European countries. The lack of guttering and drainpipes also adds to this temporary problem during periods of heavy rain in the Canary Islands. Despite having fitted a new, double glazed door, complete with threshold last year, rain still found its way inside. It is really just a question of getting the mop and putting up with it. Rain such as this occurs only for a few days each year, the sun appears again after a two or three days, and we tend to forget all about it until next time.

On days such as this, it is best to stay indoors and not attempt to drive. However, I did have an important meeting and, as the rain had eased a little, decided to take the risk. I am very pleased that I did, because I saw the most amazing and spectacular rainbow that I had only ever seen once before as a child. It was a beautiful, glistening full arc of colour, with the mountains and sea as a backdrop; it was spectacular. This was one of those occasions that we are made to feel very small and insignificant and part of some much grander overall plan.

Many years ago, as a child, camping in the Outer Hebrides off Scotland's west coast, I witnessed a beautiful rainbow, and a full arc. I ran across the fields in an effort to reach the end of the rainbow. You see, I had read somewhere that at the end of the rainbow is a crock of gold.

As I grew older, I began to understand that a rainbow is not at any specific distance, but is a phenomenon of water droplets being viewed at a certain angle. It is not 'real' in the physical sense, but is a kind of apparition, and cannot be approached physically. Rainbows can be seen whenever there are droplets of moisture in the air and the sun is shining at a low altitude angle. A similar phenomenon can be seen near fountains and waterfalls.

I remember being told at school that it is impossible to move to see a rainbow at any angle, other than one of 42 degrees from the direction opposite the Sun. Even if someone else had spotted me under, or chasing to the end of the rainbow, this second observer would have seen a different rainbow further away, but at the same angle that I had also seen it. To put it another way, it seems that a rainbow does not actually exist at a particular location in the sky. Its apparent position is dependent upon the observer's location and the position of the Sun. Confused? Yes, I was too.

So, during my childhood adventure, did I reach the end of the rainbow and discover the customary crock of gold? Sadly no. I did reach the end of the rainbow, but there was no legendary crock of gold waiting for me, and I still remember that feeling of disappointment. However, now older and a little wiser, I have come to realise that those special few minutes, witnessing a spectacular rainbow arc, with the mountains and the sea as a backdrop, was treasure enough.

Expat Attitudes

Always look on the bright side

It was time to meet up again with George for dinner. I like George, in small doses, but I do find some of his views extreme and depressing. Anyway, I am a firm believer in 'it takes all sorts to make a world' and so, after a stiff drink, I headed to the restaurant. I tend to be an optimist by nature, much preferring the view that my glass is half full, but George is the exact opposite, which does not always lead to a happy evening.

"Isn't it cold today?" grumbled George, beckoning me to sit down in front of him.

"Is it? I hadn't really noticed," I replied. "It is cooler that the 40 odd degrees we had a few weeks ago. I really don't mind it being a bit fresher."

George grunted and peered at the menu.

I sighed, and sat down. I could already sense that this was going to be a very long evening. During the next hour or so George grumbled about the state of the economy in Spain and the UK, the corruption of politicians, young people, dental implants, the European Union and the benefits that he receives in Spain.

I was tempted to point out that as he has received discretionary unemployment benefit for the over 55s from the Spanish government for the last two years, as well as free medical treatment, he didn't really have too much to complain about, but I thought better of it and bit my tongue. Suddenly, I realised that I was not going to put up with this verbal abuse of Spain any longer. I love Spain, it has been good to me and it is my home. I launched a counter attack.

Did he realise that Spain is second only to the US in terms of tourists visiting the country? Actually, the tourism sector is currently at an all time high, with 57 million visitors in a country of only 46 million people. Exports of goods and services have grown by 18 per cent in the last three years, significantly reducing the balance of trade deficit. "By the way, George, guess who is leading the Panama Canal expansion and building the first high speed train service in the Middle East between Mecca and Medina? Yes, George, you've got it, it is Spanish companies!"

George ignored my triumphant outburst and then went on to give me a tirade of distorted and inaccurate statistics about high unemployment, debt and, of course, the crisis. Didn't he know that politicians could make statistics say anything?

I countered with my own attack. "Who manages major airports around the world, and constructs off-shore wind farms in Scotland? Yes, two highly successful Spanish companies, namely Iberdrola and Repsol. Talking of off-shore wind farms, George, guess who supplies wind turbines to the world's leading economies? Who is building desalination plants in New Zealand, as well as some in desert areas? Who built the weather station for the Mars Rover? Another glass of wine, George?"

Did George realise that two Spanish banks have recently been described as two of the best banks in the world. "Did I mention Telefonica, George? Yes, I know how much you hate them after they cut you off for not paying that bill a few years ago, but they provide telecommunications services to over 300 million customers across the world and in 25 countries, including the UK and Ireland. What do you think about that?"

"Electricity bills? Yes, I know that they are high, but do you really need an electric fire on all the time in your small flat? Anyway, energy costs are still much lower than in the UK. Did you realise that 13% of our energy comes from renewable sources, such as solar where Spain is the world leader, as well as 4th in the world for wind energy? Yes, I know you hate wind turbines, George, but just think about global warming. You don't believe in it? No, I thought not. Spain is a world leader in fashion and footwear. Yes, George, I know that you only buy clothes from your local Chinese shop but..."

"Another glass of wine, George? You've had enough? Then we have the quality of our climate, food and the health care system, which, believe it or not, George, is one of the best in Europe. Yes, I know that they made a mess of your in-growing toenail, but you will live to fight another day, I am sure."

I was enjoying this, and I poured myself another glass of wine and continued my flow.

"George, did you know that Spain has the third highest life expectancy level in the world, according to the OECD? Yes, I know women live longer George, and that your wife ran off with a chiropodist from Rhyll, but that makes Spain the second highest life expectancy in the world, if we are talking about women. By the way, did you know that Spain has the highest number of organ donors in the world, with a twelve per cent increase in transplants just last year? Maybe you should think about signing up for that one day, George? More coffee, George?"

"You've had enough, and have to leave now? Oh dear. By the way, did you know that Spain is pretty good at football too? I gather it did rather well this year? OK George, good to see you too. Maybe I'll see you again one day."

Changing times for expats

The last thirty years or so have seen a rapid increase in the number of expats leaving the UK and heading for a new life in the sun. Gone are days when it was only for the likes of Eileen and Bert from Wigan, who had the cash, energy and foresight, to realise their dream of opening a bar in one of Spain's Costas. The UK's entry into the European Union, together with the right to live and work anywhere in Europe, suddenly made it possible for dreams to come true, as well as allowing the adventurous spirit of many would-be expats to be realised.

This freedom, together with the release of equity from those who were fortunate enough to own their own homes, suddenly made it possible to purchase second homes and holiday homes in a country of choice and not just by accident of birth. Early retirement for many of the fortunate, together with generous pensions and cash handouts, suddenly made everything possible.

During these 'golden years' of the property boom it seemed that there was nothing to stop the would-be expat, and many took advantage of their new found freedom. Indeed, at its peak in 2006, 22,000 pensioners emigrated from the UK to warmer locations, and where the pensioners' pound went so much further than in the UK. Many pensioners discovered a new life in the sun and, once they had acclimatised to their new surroundings, many discovered or revisited new skills and interests. Many canny pensioners also spotted new opportunities in their chosen countries and launched new businesses to accommodate the growing demand from expats.

Times have changed, and the global recession has reduced the overall number of pensioners emigrating from the UK to just 8000 in 2011. In the last few years, pensioners have found it more difficult to sell their homes in the UK, property values have fallen, and whether it is now cheaper to live in a warmer location has become more of a matter for debate than fact.

Recent statistics have revealed that 9 out of 10 people, who move overseas, do so because of their work, or the opportunity to find a permanent job in countries such as Australia, New Zealand and the US. More than half of these emigrants are professionals, such as scientists, academics, doctors and company managers, which threatens the UK's supply of highly skilled workers.

High taxation rates, climate, university tuition charges and lifestyle are all reasons quoted as reasons for moving abroad, rather than moving primarily for work. It is a delicate balance, as well as a two-sided coin, and Government policies on immigration, taxation and tuition charges, for instance, all directly affect the number of people planning to leave the UK for a more fulfilling life outside the UK, as well as for those seeking a new life and employment in the UK.

I recall some years ago, when the UK's dental service was in a state of flux, with many dentists refusing to treat National Health Service patients, and only offered treatment to private patients. For a time, there was a shortage of British dentists willing to work within the NHS. However, at the same time in Spain, too many dentists had been trained and were unable to find work. As a result, many newly qualified dentists emigrated from Spain to join NHS dental practices in the UK. Over time, this mass emigration of dentists to the UK led to a shortage of dentists in Spain, which the statisticians had not foreseen. As a result, many dentists moved to Spain from Scandinavia, as well as from South America, and particularly from Argentina, to establish new and successful dental practices in Spain.

Maybe all governments need to be more aware of the impact of short term, and apparently popular policies, designed to 'fix things' politically, as well as pleasing readers of some tabloid newspapers, and particularly those issues relating to immigration, education, health and taxation. Such short-term political fixes often have a longer term negative impact upon the prosperity, health and well being of a nation and tend to have a habit of biting back where it hurts most.

The Unsuspecting Expat

A story about a Swedish couple, Mona and Erik, who have visited Gran Canaria 70 times in the last 46 years and recently received an award from the island's government, caught my attention this week. This couple's story will jog the memories of many expats on the island, as well as expats across the world, as to the reasons why they have settled in a particular destination. For this 80-year-old Swedish couple, the draw of a welcoming, healthy and warm climate, as well as tennis and long, leisurely evenings spent with good friends has ensured their return to their favourite destination time and time again. Indeed, the couple regard Gran Canaria as their second home.

I remember this feeling so well. Many years ago, my partner and I arrived for a one-week holiday on the island, and immediately felt at home. I still remember the dread of returning to the UK and the deep longing of wanting to remain on the island forever, as I was forcibly propelled up the aircraft steps for the dreaded flight back home to the UK.

A few weeks later, we returned to the island again, and again. Each year, wherever our holiday plans took us, we would always ensure that we returned to the island for as many visits as we could afford. Eventually of course, it was a deep longing to find work and to make our permanent home on the island, which seemed impossible at the time. However, hard work and good fortune eventually brought us to our favourite destination.

I know of many people who have a deep sense of longing for a particular destination. It may be Spain's Costa Blanca, the South of France, Portugal's Algarve or maybe Thailand. It is almost as if we feel that we belong in a certain place rather than where we currently live through an accident of birth. The symptoms are easy to spot and we have many friends who seem to have caught this particular disease. It usually begins with a deep sense of longing to return to a particular destination, and the feeling, which is very hard to explain, that you are almost being drawn there. Regular holidays are just the start, and it may be that the 'holiday romance' repeated time and time again with a particular destination is all that is required. No commitment, no ties, just a sensuous flirtation and a brief affair.

However, if this 'holiday affair' evolves into several visits each year, staying at and visiting the same favourite places, eating in the same familiar restaurants, regularly collecting local magazines and newspapers "Just to see what the cost of housing is over here", the unsuspecting expat should be extremely careful as these are just some of the early symptoms of the unsuspecting expat. The danger signs are very real when they begin regularly looking at the property advertisements in newspapers and magazines. This usually extends quickly into peering longingly into the windows of estate agents, or possibly going inside to ask a few questions. Once they find that perfect spot by the beach, in the mountains, by the lake or wherever they may seek their own personal paradise, they are hooked. The best thing to do is to finally admit that they have caught the disease and just do whatever it takes to make it happen and begin to live their dream. Recognise the symptoms?

Although our Swedish octogenarian couple maintain a home in Sweden and visit the island regularly for holidays each year, it is clear that they are islanders in all but name. Mind you, Erik also pointed out that they come from Scandinavia where they live about 24 degrees below zero ... and it is very cold. "Believe me," he went on to say, "here we have a wonderful climate with a very friendly and nice people." I guess that with temperatures that cold there is a major incentive to escape to the sun.

The Cafe Bar

"I really do fancy a cup of coffee. My feet are killing me!" I complained to my partner, as we trudged around the narrow streets of a very pretty village that we had recently discovered.

"There's a cafe bar over here", he replied. Pointing to the large open doorway, I could see several very comfortable looking chairs and two large sofas and a few small tables. "It looks clean enough, lets give it a try."

We wandered inside. It looked very homely with some lovely photos and pictures of the village, and people working in it. There was one beautiful, large photo of fishermen pulling in their catch at the harbour we had just visited.

We sat on one of the comfortable sofas and eventually an old lady came over to us. She looked a little ancient to be still working, but she beamed a broad toothless smile, and we exchanged pleasantries. I ordered two coffees and asked if she had any croissants, as we had not had any breakfast. The old lady shook her head, but indicated that she could serve us with warm bread rolls, butter and marmalade instead. I nodded gratefully, and the old lady smiled, but warned me that it may take a few minutes to prepare. We were in no hurry and were pleased to have a rest. Suddenly, the elderly waitress appeared again, smiled her toothless grin, and left what appeared to be two large brandies.

We sat and relaxed. The cafe bar was very pleasant and I admired the detail of the artefacts, ornaments, photos and pictures from a bygone age. Photos of camels pulling ploughs, angelic looking, freshly scrubbed children grouped together outside the local church after their first communions, as well as many photos of fishermen long gone that adorned the walls. This little cafe bar was indeed a treasure, and we decided that we would be visiting it again very soon.

I was puzzled to see the waitress put on a shawl, pick up a basket and then disappear out of the door. She returned shortly afterwards with what, I assumed, were fresh rolls, which appeared a few minutes later, deliciously warm and placed tastefully in a basket, together with a small pot of butter, a freshly opened jar of jam, and a small daisy-like yellow flower to add the finishing touch. We thanked the waitress and told her how much we appreciated fresh rolls for breakfast. She beamed her toothless smile with pleasure, and wandered off into the kitchen.

The coffee was some of the best that we had ever tasted, and the rolls were delicious, as was the apricot jam. As I was driving, my partner polished off my brandy as well, and seemed much happier for it. We took our time, and eventually the elderly waitress positioned herself on one of the armchairs at the side of the bar, watching us carefully, smiling her toothless smile as she continued with what looked like crocheting a large shawl.

Eventually, it was time to leave. I beckoned to the waitress for the bill. She shook her head "Nada", she replied, which means "nothing". I tried again to ask for the bill, but the old lady became agitated and shook her head vigorously, followed by a babble of Spanish that I could not understand. I managed to leave a note under the saucer before we left and we thanked the elderly lady profusely for looking after us so well and assured her that we would visit her again soon. She grinned her toothless smile, nodded and waved as we left the cafe bar.

Later, during the day we met up with a friend for lunch and I told him about the very friendly cafe bar, the elderly lady and the story about how she went to the bakery to get us fresh, warm rolls.

Our friend listened, looked puzzled and then suddenly roared with laughter. "Tell me again where this bar is?" he demanded. "Did you notice a car parked inside?"

We told him that we had noticed an ancient car parked inside and at the far end of the large room. We had thought it a little strange, but assumed that it was all part of the 1950s decor. "The whole place had a 'Cuban' feel about it," I declared.

When our friend had finally finished laughing, he told us that our "Lovely little cafe bar" where we had so enjoyed our coffee, rolls and brandy that morning was, in fact, the private home of Marie-Carmen. It was not a cafe bar after all, but Marie-Carmen's integral garage, which she used as her sitting room!

Keeping in Touch

I was chatting to an elderly couple, Anne and George, in a bar the other day. It is one of the benefits of people watching in local bars; there are just so many interesting people around. They told me that they had lived in Gran Canaria for nearly thirty years, and that although they always intended to remain on the island, they still regarded the UK as home. They return to the UK once or twice a year for a month at a time, and stay with various relatives and friends. However, despite their visits, they complained that they often felt 'out of touch' and detached from the UK, and thought that their friends and relatives didn't seem interested in them or their lives anymore, or keep them involved in the way that they used to.

There is an expression that says 'Absence makes the heart grow fonder', which is neatly countered by one that says 'Out of sight and out of mind'. It is of course a human condition that although we all always mean to keep in touch with our family and friends, work and other issues often get in the way of good intentions, and it can take real effort on both sides to keep in touch.

Expats, and particularly those living in sunnier climes, often forget that the folk back home are still battling with their own problems. Stress at work, problems with the kids, and high gas and electricity bills all take their toll. Quite simply, there is often not enough time to call Mum and Dad basking in the Canary Islands. After all, on a really bad day, the thought may sometimes cross their mind that if Mum and Dad hadn't been quite so selfish and moved to the sun, they would be on hand to babysit!

I have always found that with family and best friends, even though we might not have spoken for weeks or even months, time is irrelevant. When we are next in contact, the conversation resumes as if it were only the previous day that we last spoke. However, it is always a good idea, as with all telephone conversations with the folks back home, to be aware of certain sensitivities, such as the weather. Whilst I may be basking in 27 degrees and sipping a cocktail on the sun terrace, I try to be aware that my family and friends may be trying to cope with minus 5 degrees or heavy rain, a clutch of screaming children, as well as the week's groceries.

Anne went on to tell me that they are always meticulous about phoning family and friends on Sunday afternoons each week, and they couldn't understand why their friends were often not there to answer the phone, or unable to have a lengthy chat. "We like using our videocam on Skype", she added with a flourish, and I immediately suspected that the problem was - insensitivity to others. I can think of a number of friends and relatives, although happy to use Skype by appointment, would rather not be seen unshaven, or with a towel and curlers in their hair or, in some cases, not without first having a full facial!

Sadly, Anne and George seemed oblivious that other people have busy lives. They too have things to do, people to see, crises to deal with, and rows to be resolved. Some people like the routine of regular calls but, in my experience, asking people when it is best to call is often a good idea or just try to be sensitive to times when people are working, collecting the kids from school, meal times etc. If it is difficult, use other methods of communication instead.

Personally, I prefer to use emails, text messages, WhatsApp, Twitter and Facebook to keep in contact with family and friends. Despite the lack of popularity and some cynicism from the older generation, social media has brought families and friends together. I have renewed friendship with many people since I joined Facebook and, despite the much-publicised negatives of using social networks, I find that it is one of the important factors in remaining a happy and contented expat.

A National Obsession

It is a well-known characteristic of the British psyche that we like nothing more than to complain about the weather. Usually, it is the topic of most conversations and is a national obsession. It has become even worse over recent years, prompted by the 'wall-to-wall' coverage on television and radio news. Even so, I still regard weather forecasting as little more than fortune telling, as inaccurate predictions of flooding and drought expose the many deficiencies of this 'science'. Maybe weather forecasting should be regarded as an art form instead of science?

One would think that once the Brit has become an expat, personally choosing where they should live, that would be the end of the matter. If, for example, the expat chooses to move to Scandinavia, it would not be unreasonable to expect some chilly nights from time-to-time. Thailand suffers from high humidity during parts of the year, which is best avoided if this is likely to be a problem. Northern Spain and France are also likely to be wet for parts of the year, and should make the expat wonder why he left home in the first place, whereas a move to the South of France, Southern Spain or the Canary Islands should make the sun-seeking expat feel ecstatic. Maybe not, after all there is always something else to complain about.

Life in the Canary Islands is very good overall. Not for nothing did the Greek philosopher and geographer, Ptolemy, call them 'Those Fortunate

Isles'. The climate is wonderful, with only a little occasional rain, which usually takes place in February each year. However, as these islands are just off the coast of Africa, it can get very warm at times, and even what could be described as hot for three to four days, four times each year. This occasional, yet excessive heat and dust is as a result of a 'calima' with hot winds and dust blowing from the Sahara. Temperatures can nudge 40 degrees or more and, as the locals are well aware, the best thing is to stay indoors, drink lots of fluids (non-alcoholic), generally take it easy and avoid rushing about. Air conditioning may be used if necessary, but this can bring additional problems, particularly for those with health issues. The golden rule is to be sensible and cautious.

Do all expats and tourists heed this warning? Sadly, many do not. Some will still venture to the beach and wonder why they are later hospitalised with heat exposure. Others will decide that as it is such a lovely day they will go on a long walk into the mountains. Big mistake, as several unfortunate expats do not live to tell the tale each year after such foolish exploits during high temperatures. The remaining expats, mostly British, will spend their days on Twitter and Facebook, or in local bars, complaining about the 'excessive' heat that they are coping with.

Such excesses of heat are, of course, much more serious for farmers and particularly those with livestock, and if the water supply is unable to meet demand. However, many Canarians are well aware of the regularity and sudden intensity of calimas and have had the good sense to build wells and reservoirs to cope with such emergencies, should the water supply fail which, thankfully, is rare. Indeed, builders of new homes on the islands are now obliged to install water reservoirs to provide a buffer for those occasional periods when the main water supply is disrupted.

So, back to the national characteristics of the typical British expat. We just love complaining about the weather, be it too wet, too dry, too humid, too cold or too hot - wherever we may be.

The Transitory Expat

As a newspaper reporter in Spain's Costa Blanca, I quickly came to love and admire some of my fellow expats, who were enthusiastically determined not to let old age and growing infirmity get in the way of having a really good time. Clubs and associations flourished everywhere and new ones seemed to be appearing all the time. From salsa classes, brass bands and stamp collecting to tap dancing for the over eighties, there really was something for everyone to enjoy. I sometimes wondered how they all had the energy, as we were summoned to various neighbours' terraces for "a quick drink" that rarely ended until two o'clock the following morning.

It came as some surprise when a British Consular official in the Costa Blanca announced to me during an interview that, "One must remember that the Brits come here to die." The comment astounded and puzzled me, as the evidence that I had was completely to the contrary. British expats did anything and everything but move to Spain to die. I had never seen a livelier bunch of over seventies!

I think, and hope, that what the now retired and substantially elevated consular official actually meant to say was that the majority of retired British expats in Spain move to the country as a permanent, and not a temporary, venture. Most intend to enjoy their retirement living in the sun, in a dream home, taking life easier and doing the things that they always wanted to do. Most have no intention of ever returning to the UK, and will enjoy an active retirement until they expire.

I contrast this to expat life in the Canary Islands. One of the few things that I dislike is the transitory nature of life on the islands. It is very difficult to make and keep friends who intend to stay for any length of time, and truly regard the islands as their permanent home. I know many people, after all it is a small community, but my heart sinks when I hear them talk about "going home to the UK". By the time that we get to know them as friends, it seems that most have either lost their jobs, relationships have been destroyed, they are in financial difficulties or they cannot stand the heat (in more ways than one).

Many expats realise too late that to truly enjoy life on these beautiful islands, they also have to put something back. Low pay, long hours, periods of unemployment and poor employment prospects really do have to be taken into account, and the less-than-determined expat quickly realises that there is no such thing as a free sun-bed.

Unlike the Costa Blanca, many people that we know come and go after a few months or a few years. Very few intend to stay on the islands and make it their home. Of course, there are exceptions, but these are few. If I return to the comment made by the British Consular official in the Costa Blanca, I would say that people move to the Canary Islands to work, and certainly not to die. Sadly, due to the recession, and even before the recession, there are not jobs for all and many return to the countries of origin sadder, but wiser.

We all value friendships, and I don't mean cursory acquaintances, such as the "You must call and see me sometime" brigade, but those for whom you have a genuine empathy with and feeling for. These are the people that you would do anything for and know that it would be reciprocated. True friendships are rare and I guess most of us would count ourselves fortunate if we have enough true friends to match the fingers of one hand.

Island friendships are difficult to sustain and lack the support structures of the Costa Blanca. I now often find myself subconsciously gauging just how long new friends are likely to stay the course on the islands before I invest too much time and energy in getting to know them properly. Experience tells me that within a few months or a couple of years, most will return to the land of their birth and will become just another name on a Christmas card list.

The Cynical Expat

The definition of 'cynicism' appears to have changed over the years. I have always understood the definition to be 'a sneering faultfinder', yet later definitions appear to embrace the overall discontent of modern society. It is currently a definition that refers to the belief that people are motivated by self-interest, because they are distrustful of human integrity or sincerity. Cynics are therefore distrustful of the motives of others, and are contemptuous of the human race as a whole. I find this view to be both depressing, disappointing and a likely cause of mass suicide.

Spending much of my life working with children and young people was always refreshing and exciting, because children have no understanding of cynicism. It does not come naturally to them. It is learned and spreads like a systemic poison from their elders, as they grow older.

Of course, at the right time and in the right place, cynicism can be amusing. Recently reading a couple of books by Paul O'Grady, of Lily Savage fame, there is a healthy dose of cynicism, laced with a tad of realism, but with a generous dollop of hope for the future of the human race, as well as a positive view of the human spirit. Cynicism is closely linked to sarcasm, which I also detest, and fully agree that it is the "lowest form of wit'. It is not clever and rarely amusing.

Have you noticed that many weaker comedians, as well as many Internet blogs and posts seem to thrive entirely on cynicism and sarcasm nowadays? I suspect that much of this is because it is easier to vocalise one's true feelings and frustrations about the nature of society, the recession, government and general woes, and cynicism is a simple way for the less articulate to be shrilly heard, and to let off steam. So, I guess in that sense, it does have a kind of purpose.

If you truly want to witness cynicism at its very best and loudest, the best place for it to be enjoyed is to be sitting in the haze of a British bar for expats in Spain. There you will quickly hear pure hatred, bigotry and cynicism at its delicious best, mostly fed and nurtured by regular readings of the Daily Hate. Most decent people will wince at the opinions raised about the European Union, the government (any government), race, religion, hanging and flogging, Muslims, the cabbage pickers of Lincolnshire, Nick Clegg and, above all, Spain.

I never cease to be amazed by the "my glass is half empty" brigade, where the country that has become their home in the sun is often the brunt of the "they do it better in Wigan brigade". Does Spain really owe them a living in the sun? Many expats are angry that the value of their property (if they are fortunate enough to own one) has fallen, the sun doesn't shine as much and it is too cold, or the sun shines much more and it is too hot. Many go on to express their feelings about the health service (that they have not paid into), together with a lack of pork pies and "real bacon", as they put it.

Many Brit expats refuse to learn the language, or even make an attempt at it, will only use a British tradesman, because they will be "ripped off by the Spanish" and will only visit a private British doctor if they are sick. If the truth be known, most expats will get a far better job done at a lower price by a Spanish tradesman, or better care provided by their local health centre. In addition, many simply do not understand the euro and what it stands for, and are bitterly upset when the euro gains in value against the pound.

Such expats continue to call the UK "home" and generally refuse to commit to expat life, other than to spend endless starlit nights in Brit bars. The cynical expat then wonders why it has all gone so badly wrong, they have to pack their bags and return from where they came. Once back in the UK, the failed expat can now eat as many pork pies and as much bacon as their cholesterol intake will allow, yet will continue to moan bitterly, but this time it will be about the UK, the health service, the government and how much better things were in Spain, where the sun shone. If only they had not left...

The message is clear. Be positive, make the most of new opportunities or challenges that present themselves, and above all, try to put something back. I have met so many fulfilled and happy expats in Spain, and this appears to be their secret. We all have bad and frustrating days from time to time, but even these can be exciting and provide a lesson to be learned, or how to do it better next time, and this is the true essence of expat life. As we are currently learning, many Brits are not good Europeans. However, if we really do want to make a success of expat life, let us look on the positive side, count our many blessings, adopt a "my glass is half full" attitude and, finally, cut out the moaning, sarcasm and cynicism. Most of us really do not want to hear it.

The Complaining Expat

Most expats find that from time to time they seem to be banging their heads against a concrete wall (sorry, no bricks on this island). Sometimes, it is the bureaucratic nature of the country which, to be fair, could be said about most countries where the expat doesn't fully understand the culture, language and systems. In most cases, the issues and problems faced are our own fault and caused by misunderstandings and misinterpretations of language, particularly when concerned with legal, financial and medical issues, whilst occasionally it is the sheer bloody mindedness of the bureaucrat concerned, who doesn't quite see why expats should benefit from the same rules as he and his fellow countrymen. In such cases it should be a simple process of referring the bureaucrat and his organisation to the European Union Charter, but life is never quite that simple, is it?

If simple conversation fails, I recommend asking to speak to the boss of the outfit, who is usually having a late breakfast, speaking to a client, or probably having carnal relations with his secretary in the back office. Asking for the complaints book (libro de reclamaciones) is also a good start, and causes endless amusement for the office staff witnessing your displeasure. However, please be aware that nothing ever happens, but you will feel much better for completing the form, which will ask for all kinds of irrelevant information in great detail.

Personally, I remain a great believer in the power of the good old letter of complaint. Old fashioned it may be, but it still has many useful functions, such as the surprise factor. After all, how many people do you know who still write letters? If you send a letter, at least you will appear literate and know what you are doing. It also has the power of that lovely word, gravitas, if carried out correctly.

A well-written letter far supersedes the frivolity of the phone call and unreliability of emails. After all, has anyone ever called you back when promised? It is merely something to say when the recipient of your premium rate phone call to customer services wishes to complete the varnishing of her nails, or simply cannot be bothered to walk to the far end of the office to speak to the suit in charge. Emails are, in my opinion, a real 'no, no' if you really want someone to read and act upon your complaint. It is far too easy for the intended recipient to say "Your email must have gone into spam", "Did you send it to the correct email address?" or more insultingly, "Did you remember to press the send button?" I strongly suggest, that if you wish to make an impact, you send a letter.

Firstly, ensure that your letter of complaint is well written. Cut out all the foul language, as well as repetition. Keep it brief and to the point. Ensure that a copy is translated into Spanish as well as English, and send printed copies of both versions. Do not send a hand-written letter, because copper plate and the fountain pen went out of fashion a few years ago. We are always being told that standards in English have plummeted in recent years and that most foreigners speak and write English better than most British expats. Sadly, this is mostly true; so do not give our hosts the pleasure of proving it to you.

Secondly, stretch the truth a little. Attempt to show some inside knowledge of the issue about which you are complaining. Maybe you have a contact doing similar work in another Town Hall or bank? A little name-dropping may also help in Spain. The occasional threat may also assist your cause, such as hinting that you will close your account or start a petition. Personally, I always threaten exposure in the national papers, which tends to do the trick. Whatever you do, don't threaten a 'denuncia'; this is just so passé nowadays, and your letter will merely be tossed aside with a snort.

Thirdly, always send a copy of your letter to the manager of the department concerned, with a copy to customer services at head office, marked 'Urgent'. I always send a third copy to the Chief Executive of the organisation as well, but it must be addressed to a real person, so you will have to hunt for details on the Internet. The Chief Executive may never read your letter, but you can be sure that it will be logged, just in case you are a shareholder, or someone really important. Always send letters by signed for post. It costs a little extra, but just think of the inconvenience it causes. It is well worth spending a few extra euros for this simple pleasure.

Fourthly, send a further copy by fax. The Spanish, in particular, continue to have a love affair with the humble fax machine, even though most expats popped theirs into the bin many years ago. Remember to print out the proof of sending that even the basic machines offer as standard.

Finally, never give up. If this process fails, simply repeat it, but include more people on your mailing list, such as your local councillor, trade association or ombudsman. Eventually, they will get fed up and listen. Even if they don't, the process of complaining will have given you considerable amusement, just as long as you don't take it too seriously.

The Feel Good Factor

According to recent research, the feel good factor is a rare phenomenon in the UK nowadays. However, the good news is that this research has concluded that the feel good factor is currently the highest that it has been for about three years in the UK. Maybe it is due to Andy Murray winning Wimbledon, the naughty Muslim cleric, Abu Qatada, being deported to Jordan, or maybe the economy improving a little. Whatever it is, I do wish that the UK could have much more of it, because it is always so much nicer to chat to people in the UK who do not sound as if they are about to jump from a very high building.

Of course, we all know the real reason for the current high spirits in the UK; it is the weather, of course. After a depressingly long, wet and cold winter, and a terrible spring, most people are desperate to see the sun once again and to bask in something akin to warm rays. Switching off the central heating, if fortunate enough to have it, using the barbecue purchased a few years ago and only used a couple of times, buying a summer dress or a pair of shorts all add to that feeling of well being. Summer picnics with the kids on the beach or just walking in the forest – was that all just a dream, or did it really happen when we were children, I wonder?

Like so many over a certain age, we do begin to wonder if our memories are playing tricks on us, and that our brains simply cut out those endless days of rain that we experienced during the school summer holidays. It didn't rain at all then, did it? I seemed to spend endless days playing outside, going on cycle rides, picnics and playing with friends. I also remember seeing numerous butterflies of many different colourful species, such as red admirals, tortoiseshells and peacocks. I really don't remember any rain at all during those endlessly long summer holidays.

During the last few years of living in the UK, I became aware of more people suffering from Seasonal Affective Disorder (SAD), which is basically winter depression affecting otherwise healthy people during the rest of the year. The condition is usually triggered by a lack of sunlight and is treated by light therapy and in some cases by anti depressants. However, in some cases the condition can be serious and have tragic consequences.

Since moving to Spain and the Canary Islands, I quickly dropped my usual habit of checking the weather each morning, as it was no longer necessary. In the Canary Islands, for instance, it is mostly warm throughout the year. We may get some cloud from time to time, which normally clears by mid morning, or a calima that boosts the heat rapidly for a few days, but generally, we can have a barbecue when we would like one, we don't need rain coats and central heating issues are usually addressed by the lighting of one or two or candles during a winter's evening if we feel a little chilly. However, should the heat become a little excessive, which it may do in August, then air conditioning is a necessity.

This desperate need for the 'feel good factor' is one of the many driving forces that persuade many would-be expats to finally accept that they may be in the wrong country for their health and general well being. They gradually realise that they need to make the most of the time that they have. Usually, this means escaping from the cold and wet weather and heading for a life in the sun. For some, this may not be possible, and with the global recession, opportunities to move to another country now seem much more problematic, with even European countries being less welcoming than they were to expats a few years ago. However, there are still many opportunities for those who have the determination and foresight, and like a challenge, to succeed.

Our fingers are crossed for our friends and relatives that the true summer weather that is currently being enjoyed in the UK and mainland Europe continues for a long time to come, but then again there is always the issue of drought rearing its ugly head to spoil things if it lasts for too long. Meanwhile, enjoy summer barbecues, tea on the patio, Wimbledon and strawberries and fresh cream.

Legal and Working Challenges

The
Canary
Islander

What a Catastral!

Expats who have bought, or are planning to purchase, a home in Spain (or France) need to know about the Catastral. This term is often assumed to be very similar to the UK's Land Registry, which records legal ownership of a property, which it is not. In Spain, the Catastral (or if in France, the Cadastre) is merely an estimate of the value of the property and is used for that most important of functions, determining the taxes that should be paid.

The base figure for the Catastral is determined in a number of ways, which are complicated to understand. Broadly speaking, the value of the property is decided by government employees, who use complex valuation guidelines that are based upon the description of the property, as well its use. In addition, licence applications, observations from aerial photos (so beware if you plan to add an additional room for Granny!), the site's registered boundaries, historical records, planning and licence applications, title deeds and agricultural 'parcelas'.

The calculation is not always without problems, as additions to the building, such as another bedroom, integral garage and other alterations will affect the value of the property and may take some time to catch up, as will the bill for the missed property taxes. It should also be understood that the details for the Catastral and the 'Nota Simple' are obtained in different ways, and therefore the final figures may be very different.

You may be wondering why I am so interested in this issue. Well, since we moved into our new property in 2006 we have been in the delightful situation of never having paid a cent in property taxes. For some, this may be a matter for celebration, but the realists amongst us will realise that, as with death, taxation is never truly escaped, just put off for a while. The time for paying our taxes to the Town Hall has come and gone each year and, despite regular visits to the Town Hall asking for a bill, we have never received one. However, we have received many promises, which usually included blaming the builder, staff holidays, staff births and staff deaths, together with the Town Hall being evacuated because it was falling down (best to avoid the Municipality architect in future!), but no tax bill has ever arrived.

However, I am now pleased to report that on 2 January a very nice policeman on a motor cycle, sporting a rather worrying gun at his side, arrived at our home and presented us with a bill for property taxes since 2006. He kindly went over all the details, warning us that it must be paid by 2 February otherwise we would be shot. I thanked him, and offered him a mince pie, which he declined. However, he did wish us a "Happy New Year" with a broad smile, before he kick started his moped and sped away. I was very impressed that we had received such a personal service; we never received this quality of service from the good people at Bournemouth Town Hall. However, I suspect that in these financially stringent times, our policeman's salary rather depended upon us paying the bill sooner rather than later. No wonder he was so charming.

We are now in the proud possession of a bill for seven year's worth of property taxes. I really do wish that I had put money aside each year, as originally planned, in preparation for this fateful day. I headed for a coffee and a large brandy to recover. What a start to the New Year.

The Exceptionally Long and Highly Irritating Scarf

Bureaucracy is unique to a particular country and culture. I am told that it is blisteringly efficient in Germany, painfully slow in Italy and Greece, and in France... well, it is best not to even raise the subject with the locals. For most expats living in Spain, bureaucracy is just one of those things that we have to put up with, and is the downside to a mostly very pleasant lifestyle. Most of us have had showdowns and brushoffs with a variety of officials from Government departments, Police, Town Halls, Traffic and Customs departments. Not only is it the seemingly pointless myriad of paperwork that has to be dealt with, but that the requirements continually change, which even the administrative staff are often unaware of.

A recent visit to my local Town Hall was a case in point. I had to obtain a copy of the Padron (certificado de empadronamiento). I have requested this document from various Town Halls for the use of a number of government departments on endless occasions over the years. Sometimes the department in question requires the Padron, together with an original residency certificate; sometimes they require a photocopy, because they will not produce one for you. They may require it to be certified by a notary, or maybe the police. In all cases, there are different requirements and all will result in at least a second visit to the department concerned and several hours queuing. In this age of instantaneous communication,

I often wonder why one official in one department cannot merely click onto the website of another government department and collect all the information that they want in an instant. I guess that is just too obvious and would take the fun out of the pointless game that we all play.

Just one tip, never, never reveal all your paperwork to the clerk at the early stages. It's a little like revealing all your cards too early in the game. Keep them well hidden in a bag below their range of sight, or stuffed into the back of your trousers or bra. Spanish officials are drawn like magnets at the very sign of paper. They just adore it, and will whisk away anything that they may see about your person before you can say "Mañana" and will never be seen again.

I joined the queue of another eighteen people at the Town Hall, duly armed with photocopies of my documents, notarised copies, as well as some stamped by the police. I had my passport, driving licence, and copies of all documents. Together with my survival pack of sandwiches, a packet of Kendal Mint Cake, a bottle of water and a picnic chair, I felt that, apart from a call of nature, I was sufficiently well prepared to spend the entire day at the Town Hall, if necessary.

The one clerk on the desk was coping remarkably well. Unusually, he was listening attentively to questions posed by his customers, entering data on a computer, bonking sheets of paper and sending near completed clients to the adjacent ticket machine to pay for those very special documents. I admired his multitasking skills, but I did wonder what exactly the eight colleagues sitting at the desks behind him were doing. One or two were peering vaguely into computer screens, others were sipping water and chewing gum, one was busily filing her nails whilst one very elegant, yet irritating woman, wearing an exceptionally long and highly irritating scarf, wandered from desk to desk. From time to time she would deliver an occasional sheet of paper, flicking her scarf behind her. Occasionally, she would wander to the counter to chat to a customer that she recognised, but never once attempted to help the over burdened counter clerk or do anything useful other than trying to look elegant in that exceptionally long and highly irritating scarf when it was already 27 degrees on hot and sunny February day.

Eventually I reached the counter clerk. I politely made my request in well-rehearsed Spanish. He nodded, bonked a sheet of paper and waved me to a machine where I had to pay my three euros. In the 90 minutes that I had been waiting, I calculated that the clerk had taken around 200 euros in fees. As the German gentleman in front to me commented, "You would think that with such high employment in Spain, the Town Hall would find it useful to employ at least two more counter staff. It would save unemployment benefit, and they would pay for themselves in a few hours. Personally, I was thinking more of immediate redundancy for the lady with the exceptionally long and highly irritating scarf.

Meringues and Penguins

So, where would you like to get married? OK, you are already married, don't want to get married, or unlikely to be asked to get married. Let's not let detail get in the way of a good story.

In the old days, of course, a wedding meant a trip to the local registry office if you were a film star, eloping, a criminal, or just a cheapskate. Alternatively, you could go for the full bells and whistles routine, penguin suits and top hats, together with a gorgeous bride and bridesmaids, all resembling large, fluffy meringues, for that special day of your dreams.

One of the most unusual weddings that I have witnessed was a few years ago, whilst sitting in a bar in Ibiza overlooking a very beautiful beach. Those of you who are familiar with the music from Cafe del Mar will know what I am taking about when I refer to the most incredible sunset accompanying both cocktails and great music. On this particular evening, an unusual wedding was also taking place on the beach below our cafe bar. Indeed, we were two of the uninvited guests and remain deeply penitent to this very day for attending a wedding in floral shorts. I shudder to think what the wedding photos looked like.

The ceremony was simple, with not a meringue or penguin suit in sight. Indeed, in today's parlance, I would say that the wedding was exceptionally cool. It was sincere, appeared deliciously simple, yet no doubt cost a fortune, which is always the clever illusion, indulged by those who really do have money. Fire-eaters, jugglers and exotic dancers completed the illusion of stylistic perfection, which was clearly the theme of the entire event. I can also personally vouch for the generosity of the bride's father, as we shared several glasses of rather lovely champagne with the happy couple, as did most of the holidaymakers on the terrace who, like ourselves, were uninvited yet enthusiastic guests and witnesses of the great day.

It was the following day, when I was nursing a splendid hangover, that we were told that the newly married couple were film stars of some considerable importance. However, after all the beautiful champagne and canapés that generously found their way to our table, I am sworn to secrecy for all time as to the couple's true identity. It is a promise that I intend to keep, as I understand that there are Mafia connections not to be trifled with.

I mention this encounter, because I have heard that the good people working in the Directorate General of Costas in my municipality of San Bartolome de Tirajana in Gran Canaria are still refusing to allow couples to marry on our islands' beautiful beaches. Permission has been requested, licences have been applied for and we have a marvellous opportunity to earn some much needed euros from the rich and famous who would like to take advantage of our wonderful climate and facilities for the perfect wedding.

We have wonderful weather for most of the year and, as a bonus, we can also offer sand in a variety of colours. Although real volcanic sand is the norm, we can also offer brilliant white sand for those brides in brilliant white wedding dresses, imported specially at great expense, both economic and environmental, from the Caribbean. In short, Gran Canaria has it all, and is the perfect wedding destination.

Personally, I cannot see why our elected officials have not yet granted permission. After all, does it really matter whether one decides to get married in church, registry office, on the top of a mountain, in a lighthouse or on a beach? Getting married in a meringue dress, penguin suit, jeans or t-shirt doesn't really matter either. What really matters is love, and the long-term commitment of support and care for each other. However, as a warning, couples intent on getting married on the beach should be aware of its close proximity to rocks. Do they really want a marriage to be on the rocks before it has even started?

The Russians are Coming!

It is fascinating to look at the origins of expats moving to the Canary Islands over the last two centuries or so. In the nineteenth and twentieth centuries it was the British who stamped an almost colonial footprint on the city of Las Palmas de Gran Canaria and the north of the island. We can still see epitaphs, such as the British Church, British Cemetery and British street names dedicated to the great and good of the city at that time, and who brought great prosperity to the island in the form of shipping bananas and other fruit and vegetables to the UK. Cruise ships also regularly plied their trade to these islands, bringing with them a privileged few to enjoy these much favoured and popular "Fortunate Isles".

In later years, it was Tenerife that found the greatest favour with British holidaymakers and expats, and who still flock in great numbers to its shores. However, it was its neighbour, Gran Canaria, which attracted more discerning German holidaymakers and expats.

The reunification of Germany, following the collapse of the Berlin Wall, together with a joint taxation agreement between Germany and Spain, forced many cash strapped German expats, as well as those with holiday homes, to sell their homes. Many British purchasers, who found themselves with more ready cash than anticipated, due to rapidly rising domestic house prices on the home market, were happy to take full advantage of a property market that was rapidly falling in value.

We are now at another stage in the on going transition of the island. Since the world recession of 2008, many traditional purchasers of properties in Spain and the Canary Islands, such as the British and Irish, have been forced to sell their homes, often at much reduced prices. Scandinavians, and particularly Norwegians, whose strong currency has allowed many to view the purchase of a holiday home on the island as a rather pleasant alternative to buying the traditional summer cabin in the Norwegian lakes and mountains, have swiftly taken their place.

These islands are a wonderful patchwork of nationalities, colour, religion and race that live and work harmoniously together for most of the time. Interestingly, there is a significant Korean population on the islands, which occurred by accident following the sudden collapse of the Korean whaling industry. Hundreds of workers and their families were stranded on the island, which quickly became their home. Chinese and Indian business owners also maintain a significant presence on the island, which I strongly suspect the islands could not do without.

The identity of the islands continues to change, as it is now the Russians who are buying properties in great numbers in the Canary Islands, as well as in the Costa Blanca and Costa del Sol. In Tenerife, for instance, many companies are now sending their employees on Russian language courses, in order to better serve the needs of their new affluent clients. Indeed, it is reported that the Government is considering the relaxation of Spanish residency laws to Russians who purchase a property of sufficient value to gain automatic residency. It is thought that this measure would help to reinvigorate property sales in the country.

Personally, I have no problem with who my neighbours are, just as long as they obey the laws, traditions and culture of the country that they are in. However, I have recently received disturbing accounts from several residents who are desperately trying to sell their homes, both in the Canary Islands and in the Costa Blanca, and who are being taken advantage of by potential Russian purchasers who, it would seem, are not the most straightforward of clients to deal with.

Initially, great interest is shown in a particular property, which is nearly always one of high value. Usually there are several visits, as well as friendly attempts to get to know more about the seller. The unsuspecting seller agrees a purchase price, a deposit is paid and a date with the notary arranged. It is at the notary stage, when the attitudes of the purchaser suddenly change for the worst. The buyers, who previously appeared happy and content with the proposed deal, now suddenly find many problems with their intended purchase, including unforeseen planning and building issues, documentary and legal errors to which the seller is completely unaware until the moment of signing in the notary's office. In all cases, the prospective purchasers have insisted upon a massive reduction in the agreed purchase price before they will complete the sale. In one case that has been reported to me, the final reduction was in excess of 50,000 euros before the sale was finally and reluctantly agreed. Sadly, in all the cases reported to me, the would-be purchasers were Russian.

Some may call this good business practice, as it is the responsibility of the seller to be fully aware of the facts before the completion of the sale. Personally, I see it as sharp practice at best, and fraudulent at worst. Sellers are at their weakest position at this point in the sale, and the well-prepared buyer, with less than generous intentions, knows it. Many sellers are selling their properties because they are in financial difficulties, and wish to sell their home and move back to the UK, whilst others are trying to complete the purchase of another property to which they are already financially committed. Sellers are also at a considerable disadvantage because of language issues, and the legal 'slickness' of the purchasers' lawyers. I also wonder about the impartiality of notaries in such circumstances; they should have the power to intervene and review such transactions, but it appears that they do not do so.

It seems that all is not well on the current Russian front, and I suspect that the few accounts that have been reported to me are just the 'tip of the iceberg'. I would be interested to hear of any similar situations from readers.

Trying to 'Live the Dream'

I often receive emails from readers, and although I cannot always answer them I do what I can to help if possible. One email in particular, that I received a few days ago, has stayed in my mind. I did reply, but I fear that my reply may have been unduly negative and, I guess, unwelcome.

The email was from a young man called Paul, who was in his early twenties, living in the North of England with his partner's parents. He was out of work and clearly disillusioned with living conditions in his home town, as well as the weather. Well, most of us will understand that one. His answer was to escape to the Spanish sunshine or the Canary Islands. Well, so far, Paul and I are on a similar wavelength.

It was the next part of the message that concerned me. As well as not having a job or qualifications in the UK, he also had a partner who was seven months pregnant. He felt that the change would "do her good" as the weather was getting her down, and wondered if I knew whether he would be able to get a job during the "slow season" in the Canary Islands. I could confidently reply that there really is no "slow season" here; we get all sorts of visitors throughout the year, and you can almost determine which month it is from the visitors. For instance, the Scandies appear in October and stay until April, the Wrinklies appear in June and stay until Christmas, and the Gays are here for Carnival and Gay Pride during February, March and May, and rapidly disappear as soon as the school holidays begin. From July until September, family visitors appear from all parts of Europe, with Spanish families, mostly from Madrid, overtaking the number of other European visitors during the peak summer months.

As well as not having a job, or indeed a particular qualification or skills, the situation with Paul's partner concerned me. Clearly there would be no access to free health cover as pregnancy, unless it is linked to emergency complications, would not qualify as an emergency, which would provide free health care. Paul would not qualify for unemployment or social security, and I had a vision of this little family camping out on a beach somewhere, relying on charitable handouts.

Maybe this is OK if you are young, free and single, but not with a family. Paul told me that he had never visited the islands, but had seen a film about it, which is maybe not the best way of finding out about a new place to live. He went on to ask me about the opportunities and costs of renting a small apartment, and added that he had seven thousand pounds in the bank that would help for a while. Maybe, that is a nice sum to have for emergencies, but that amount would not last long without a job, new baby, expenses and an apartment to rent.

Sadly, I replied that, in my view, maybe the time was not right for Paul and his partner to seek a new life in the sun. Maybe they should wait for a few years, visit the islands to see if they really like it and save more money before they took the plunge. Above all, try to secure a job before they committed themselves to a move. I suspect that my reply will fall on deaf ears, and I guess I would be the same if I really wanted to do something.

This email was by no means unique, and I am concerned that the temptation of a new life in the sun for some may just be one step too far in current economic circumstances. It is also clear that because of the recession, many opportunities that I and many other expats have enjoyed in the past are being denied to the next generation who may wish to tread the same path. Without being unduly pessimistic, the expat dream has turned sour for many expats, and I hope that, in time, more opportunities will once again present themselves to a new generation of expats looking to 'Live the Dream'.

What's in it for me?

I fondly recall one expat from a few years ago who ran a thriving business in the Canary Islands, until greed finally overcame common sense and the business, somewhat predictably, failed. I enjoyed Peter's company, but became continually irritated by what became his catch phrase of "What's in it for me?" Any ideas for promotion, additional services for customers, developing good relations with the Town Hall, which is an essential part of business life in Spain, and even charitable events always met with the same predictable response of "What's in it for me?"

I appreciate that businesses are not charities, and a good businessman is always seeking opportunities to develop and expand the business and not to indulge in too many favours and freebies. However, a focus upon a philosophy based solely around "What's in it for me" is not a good strategy. The most effective and profitable businessmen that I know in both Spain and the Canary Islands are 'people' people. That is to say that these businessmen and women actually appear to like people, and doing business with them always appears to be a pleasure.

In Spain, as well as other Latin countries, it is not what you know, but who you know that is important. Successful businessmen and women in Spain and the Canary islands are part of a wide and fluid social network, and will quickly go out of their way to get to know those in power or positions of influence, yet give the impression that they do not care about such issues. Political loyalties too are also very flexible, although I suspect that being pragmatic would be the preferred term. Under no circumstances would they admit to any idea of "What's in it for me?" even though that may be the hope and eventual outcome.

Developing good relations with the local Town Hall and politicians is also something that many expat businessmen forget to cultivate. These are small islands and everyone knows everyone else, as well as much of their business. Uncomfortable it may be, but it can also work to one's advantage. I recall having a conversation with a lawyer several years ago about a property that I was interested in. Within minutes I had been introduced to the manager of a local bank, with whom I had no previous contact, and offered a mortgage without the bank knowing anything about me, simply because the lawyer played golf with the manager of the bank, and the bank manager's father in-law happened to own the property company of the house that I was interested in purchasing. Not only did I receive a free lunch, but also a favourable price and a 'special' mortgage interest rate. I have never known a transaction to proceed as smoothly and as quickly as that one.

I suspect that a lack of awareness of the hidden agenda is where many expats fail when trying to establish a business in Spain and the Canary Islands. When opening a cafe bar, for instance, it may be more appropriate to turn a blind eye to the bill for a coffee and tapas when dealing with the local police, than to present a bill. In turn, a blind eye will often be shown when opening hours are accidentally exceeded or a customer is caught smoking inside the bar. I recall one example when Peter presented a bill for a round of drinks to a group of off duty policemen who were drinking in his bar one evening. Peter became very angry when, a few days later, he was reminded by the same group of policemen that he was infringing local laws and liable to a heavy fine by having too many tables and chairs on his outside terrace. I am not suggesting that expats indulge in bribery and accept corruption, but adopting a little sensitivity to the local culture is often a wise course of action. You see, favours are repaid in kind over here and the wise expat quickly understands and accepts this.

Expats and Travel

The
Canary
Islander

Sky High Wi-Fi

Regular readers of 'Twitters' will know that I am not a great admirer of a certain low cost airline that operates in the Canary Islands. Although appearing to offer great value at first glance, by the time that the intending traveller has negotiated the complicated website, which appears intended to trick rather than reassure, paid extra for baggage, surcharges, worked out how to say "No" to the insurance offer as well as denying the "Special hand luggage that meets our specifications" offer. I find that I am already dreading the flight. Added to this, the undignified dash across the runway, a policy of not knowing whether I will be seated next to my partner or not, told that I cannot bring any duty free in addition to my hand luggage... I could go on.

The last time I flew with them I arrived at the airport for a three-week trip, and I was told that I would have to pay an additional 40 euros, as my suitcase was one kilogramme overweight. I was already in a less than amused mood when I realised that because we had to stop at Madrid on our way to Gatwick, we would be charged the baggage fee twice for our suitcases. However, in fairness, to the cabin crew, I do find that once we are in the air, the flight is generally on time and trouble free. It is just the pre flight part that is the problem. Needless to say, after our last experiences, we decided never to travel with them again, unless there was no other choice.

Enter a new airline, Norwegian. I have to say that, so far, I am most impressed. Good value no-nonsense flight bookings, an approach of 'what you see is what you get', together with a good, clear website made all the difference when I booked our next flights to the UK. We also have numbered seats, as well as the offer of free Wi-Fi and phone calls on board. We shall see what happens on board and just as long as we don't have to provide our own fuel, I guess it will be a vast improvement on the other lot.

It is the offer of free Internet whilst 30,000 feet in the air that intrigues me, as well as the possibility of making free phone calls. Without being too cynical about the offer, I seem to remember one stewardess being rather unpleasant when she realised that I had, by mistake, left Wi-Fi switched on for my iPad, as well as another passenger being warned that he would be ejected from the cabin if he didn't switch off his mobile. The reason given was that it would interfere with the plane's circuitry and that we would drop from the sky, and where we would we be then? I didn't respond, as I assumed that she was being rhetorical. Apparently, use of a mobile phone is forbidden and cabin crew have the power to shoot anyone breaking the rules. Well, it seems that they have different rules in Norway, and I shall surf to my heart's content and deal with all my emails on the flight back to the UK. After all, who can possibly be away from email and text messages for four hours? Unthinkable.

I also received another message from the Norwegian airline the other day reminding me to download their iPhone App so that I can make free calls on board. Now this offer rather alarmed me. Flights are often noisy enough if you are unfortunate enough to be seated next to a group of badly behaved adults, let alone their children, but can you imagine endless conversations of "Hello Mum, I'm on the plane! Yes, I said, I'm on the plane! Can you hear me? I'm on the PLANE!" from 300 odd passengers? I fear that days of a quiet read, together with a nap on the plane after a drink and sandwich are fast disappearing.

Cycling in the Canaries

As a child, I really hated cycling, which was mainly because of the two-mile cycle ride to the bus stop each morning. I know that memories play tricks on us, but it always seemed to be raining. Added to this, being the third child with a long gap between my eldest brother and myself, I inherited an old bone shaker of a bike. I am sure it was of the pre-war variety, black, boring and solidly built to last a lifetime. I guess it is already in a museum somewhere, standing right next to a Penny Farthing. Sadly, it was nothing like the shiny new one that my best friend, Jeremy, had been given for Christmas.

Living in the Canary Islands, I am now all for two-wheeled transport. The Tour de France, the Olympics, as well as cycling heroes such as Bradley Wiggins and Lance Armstrong (well, maybe forget the last one) have all added to the culture that present day cycling can be health promoting, fun and cool - all at the same time. It is fascinating to see the range of designer gear that one is supposed to wear before even starting to pedal nowadays. Sexy, brilliant coloured lycra, snazzy helmets, gloves and water bottles all add to the pleasure of present day cycling. Thankfully, long gone are the days when a brilliant yellow oilskin draped across head and top half of the body and cycle, passed for the latest in fashion for cyclists, as well as providing a small amount of wind and rain protection. Exactly what was the point of having a dry shirt and blazer, when my trousers, socks and shoes remained soaking wet all day?

Cycling is very popular with German and Scandinavian visitors to the island, most of whom bring their cycles with them. A determined lot they are too, and many can be seen peddling furiously along the busy roads of Gran Canaria in packs just after breakfast. I am told that many are practicing for the various races and events that they will be entering throughout the year, and cycling in almost guaranteed island sunshine for much of the year helps to increase their levels of fitness for the big races. However, all is not well for residents and non-cycling visitors to the island who have to cope with the hundreds of cycling enthusiasts that visit each year.

I can guarantee that on most mornings when I attempt to drive from my home after breakfast, I will encounter a group of twenty or thirty cyclists peddling furiously ahead of me. It would be fine if they cycled in small groups, either singly or even in pairs, but in recent weeks I have witnessed many a close shave with cars, buses and lorries, when cyclists are bunched together in groups of twenty or thirty cycles, often cycling three abreast and sometimes even holding arms or shoulders. Now, I am all for demonstrating affection for those that we love, but is it really necessary to hold hands on a busy road when cycling?

To cyclists visiting the island, may I suggest that you select some of the less busy roads, and maybe head into the mountains where you will get real exercise peddling up the steep inclines. It will be even more health promoting, but just be careful of the steep bends on the way down. Also, however much you adore your cycling partners, is it really necessary to stay glued to their backsides for the whole journey, despite their appealing lycra? Holding arms and indeed hands, is also very nice, but not on a busy road with cars, lorries and buses bombing along at 80 km/h plus. Finally, do split up a little, into groups of two or three. Forget that you are pack animals, but just prearrange a get together at a bar somewhere later during the day. You can do all the group bonding that you want to then.

Finally, make no mistake, we really do love seeing you and your euros over here, but with a little thoughtfulness before you pedal away into the sunset, do remember that you will stand an even better chance of entering those competitions back home in one piece, as well as returning to see us again next year.

The Good Luck Charm

I am always interested to hear what prompts people to leave the country of their birth to become an expat in another country. Often it is due to work commitments, or simply a desire to escape to the sun, and where maybe the retirement pound will stretch further. Sometimes people tell me that it is a book or a film that has inspired them, or set the seed for a dream that later turns into reality. It was a conversation along these lines that prompted one expat to suggest that I include a list of 'Top Films for Expats' on my Expat website and mobile Apps.

As I reflected on this suggestion, I dusted down an old copy of the film 'Tea with Mussolini', which I had not seen for many years. If you haven't seen it, you really should, because although it is set in wartime Italy, there are characters in the film that portray much of what you should not do or be as an expat, and displaying a heady mixture of Empire arrogance and paternalism that is both amusing and infuriating. Indeed, the story is not that far from reality as I have met many such characters in the last few years, both in Spain and the Canary Islands in my role as a newspaper reporter, who would be an ample match for the expat Brits in this film! Thankfully, they are now a dying breed.

It was whilst carrying out research for this new project, that another friend suggested that I add 'Little Buddha' to my list of suggested films for expats. This was not a film that I have seen, and it was whilst researching the plot on the Internet that I received a message from a friend in the Costa Blanca. His mother, Anne, had arrived in the Costa Blanca for a visit, but before she had left, a well-meaning friend had given her a small Buddha as a good luck charm. Sadly, shortly after receiving and carefully packing the Buddha in her suitcase, Anne had a large glass of coke poured all over her, ruining her new white blouse. Upon her arrival in Spain, Anne tripped and fell outside the airport, badly bruising her knee and arm, as well as her dignity and a new 200 euro pair of designer sunglasses. Not a good start to Anne's holiday.

Since Anne arrived in Spain, it has rained incessantly, and the only time that Anne ventured outside was ruined when she caught and broke the heel of her new pair of designer shoes in a drain cover outside the apartment. The following morning, when Anne awoke, she switched on her bedside lamp, which promptly exploded, shattering glass all over her. Thankfully, Anne was unhurt, but beginning to wish that either she or the Buddha had stayed at home. I am not a great believer in the effectiveness of good luck charms, other than occasionally wishing that those who have a rabbit's paw as a good luck charm have similar luck as the poor rabbit. Maybe Anne should begin to question the motives of her friend when she arrives home. Perhaps the friend was jealous and really wanted a holiday in Spain too? By the way, I understand that the good luck charm is now floating somewhere in the Mediterranean, so if you should happen to find it, I suggest that you keep well away.

Meanwhile, I continue my search for films that have proved to be an inspiration for the intending expat. I now have a rapidly growing list, but if you have any suggestions, do please let me know.

The Mañana Factor

It was very early one morning when I received a telephone call from a helpful lady, who claimed that she was from "the removals company". Apparently, they had several boxes of items belonging to me, which they would like to deliver to our home later that morning. Would I be in?

I agreed, but was taken by surprise and did not think to ask any further questions. This was a call that I had not been expecting. After all, we had moved to the island some eight years earlier, and that was the last I had anything to do with any removals company. My mind went back to ten years earlier.

Ten years ago, after we had decided to move to the Costa Blanca, we had to make another major decision. Would we, like so many expats, sell, give away and otherwise dispose of most our UK belongings, and buy all new items for our new Spanish home? Alternatively, would we take most of our UK furniture and belongings with us, which was the more expensive option? We decided that as we wanted to have our memories with us it would be money well spent. Despite this, it still meant many trips to the local charity shops to dispose of unwanted books, records, clothes and kitchen items. It was a heart breaking process in many ways, and I was relieved when my work took me away from home during those final stages of the big clear out.

Our furniture and belongings eventually arrived in the Costa Blanca, mostly unscathed apart from a broken mirror, which probably explained some of our initial periods of bad luck, although I am not at all superstitious. Surprisingly, most of the furniture fitted into our new home very well, although my electric trouser press caused some raised eyebrows, as I rarely wore a suit or long trousers. During those initial months in Spain, it was comforting to be surrounded by familiar items from our UK home, as well as items that had been in both our families for many years.

Two years later, we were once again on our travels and we arranged for all our belongings to be shipped to the Canary Islands. This was an expensive process, but we reasoned that as we had already brought everything with us to Spain, we had better complete the task and transport it all to the Canary Islands.

Upon our arrival, some of the items were to be delivered to our new, but temporary apartment, with the remainder being held in storage until we found a home that we really liked. Eventually, the remaining items were delivered to our new home, which we hoped would be the last move for a very long time. It was good to be surrounded once again by familiar items, a grandfather clock that my father had lovingly crafted many years ago, my Great Aunt Ada's china cabinet, as well as a collection of other items that mean so much to both of us.

During the intervening years, my partner and I have often had heated discussions, along the lines of

"Where is my collection of Shakespeare records?" or "Where is that ostrich egg that we brought back from South Africa?" Two glass shelves from Great Aunt Ada's china cabinet had also disappeared, as had the key to Granny's clock, as well as a number of cassette tapes. It was irritating that our highly efficient wine bottle foil cutter from California had also disappeared, as well as several videos, including 'Tea with Mussolini', which should incidentally be compulsory viewing for any intending expat on how not to approach a new life abroad. I had just assumed that my partner had disposed of these items quietly, whilst I had been working away from home during those final days in the UK.

The doorbell rang and I answered it with anticipation of what I would discover. Without a word of apology or explanation, the young man in overalls gently placed two large cardboard boxes in our driveway. I tried to ask for an explanation of why it had taken eight years to deliver the two boxes, but was answered with a broad smile, a shrug and, I think, just a hint of a wink.

Yes, most of the missing items were there. However, we no longer have a record player to play the Shakespeare records on, a video recorder to play the videos or a cassette player to play the cassettes. Great Aunt Ada's glass shelves were there, as was the key to Granny's clock, although we are still looking for the foil cutter.

Over the years I have come to accept the truism that time moves at a different pace in Spain and the Canary Islands. Generally, I now have a greater tolerance and acceptance of delays and promises, knowing that it usually works out in the end. However, I do think that a delay of eight years is pushing it.

The One Way Ticket to Paradise

Tour companies are strange and unique creations. Browsing through brochures or skipping through the pages of Internet travel sites is one of those deliciously exciting things to do during those endless cold, wet winter evenings. It is a time when we can dream of sun drenched beaches, sparking white sands and beautiful evenings sitting in a favourite bar enjoying the sunset with our favourite tipple.

Is it really like this? Well, for many it is. However, I have lived and worked long enough in tourist resorts, mingling and chatting with tour operators and visitors to realise that there is a rather more chilling side to our overseas holidays. It is an area that no one will talk about. For instance, just what does happen if you or your beloved should happen to die abroad?

Obviously death on holiday is not one of the features advertised in your glossy holiday brochure, but as inconvenient and thoughtless as it is, it really does happen and with alarming regularity too; indeed, tour companies have departments dealing solely with such issues. The stress of flights, dashing across the runway, over-relaxation (yes, there really is such a thing), too much rich food, too much alcohol, too much sun and, basically too much of everything can lead to strokes, heart attacks and much worse.

Indeed, I know of several people on our holiday islands that specialise in getting you back to the UK in one piece, albeit dead or alive, in a box or in an urn. If one is dead, one can usually assume that there will be a rather speedier check in, better quality service, less crowding, no passport control, no screaming kids, but sadly no in-flight meal either. All very reassuring, isn't it?

Death really does happen on our holiday island. I heard of one very sad true story recently of a couple that came on holiday to enjoy the sun, which I will share with you.

Sadly, the wife passed away during an unfortunate incident at a display of flamenco dancing, with the added attraction of a fire-eating act, at a high quality hotel. It was a tragic combination of too many pina colada cocktails and an unfortunate experience with a cocktail cherry that led to the good lady's early demise. She was pronounced dead as a doormat by the attending physician, and taken away to the local mortuary. It was a shocking end to a wonderful evening and fellow guests wondered how they would get through the remainder of their holidays. However, they found ways to cope with their grief.

The poor lady's husband continued to enjoy his much needed break and as he was 'all inclusive' he took advantage of every breakfast, lunch and dinner on offer, as well as all the evening shows, excursions to the local market and free cocktails until it was time for his departure to the UK. He packed his bags and took the courtesy coach to the airport and duly checked in for his flight to Gatwick.

It was a few days later when the tour company received an anxious telephone call from the mortuary that was holding the body of his dear, but very dead wife. Sadly, the holidaymaker had returned home without making arrangements for the disposal or return of his wife. So, the tour company really were left 'holding the body'.

Such things happen on holiday, so do please make sure you have a discussion about "What happens if..." before you leave home. Quality insurance cover, together with a decision about burial, cremation or burial at sea is always a good idea and does add a little 'spice' to holiday planning. Above all, do have a relaxing and enjoyable holiday!

Travel Insurance - Are you covered?

Listening to recent revelations in the UK about staff at one of the UK's major banks currently dealing with claims for the mis-selling of personal protection insurance did not surprise me. Reportedly, staff were told to automatically decline claims on their first presentation, on the basis that most people fail to pursue the issue further. This reminded me of a recent problem that I had with a major bank in Spain.

For many years I have had a gold credit card, issued by my Spanish bank, which I rarely use. When the time came for its renewal I considered cancelling it to avoid the hefty annual charge, and I discussed this with a member of staff at my local branch. Needless to say, I was advised to keep the card on the basis that it provided me with valuable additional services, such as travel and accidental damage insurance. As I also take out an annual travel insurance policy to cover my partner and myself during our visits to the UK and elsewhere, the bank suggested that I no longer needed this as I was duplicating the cover with that already provided by the gold card, assuming that I used it to book the tickets. To me, it made good financial sense to accept my bank's advice to continue with the card, and to not renew the travel insurance policy.

A few months later, I booked flights and hotel accommodation with my gold card for my partner and myself to visit the UK. My partner was taken ill and hospitalised, and we were subsequently warned not to fly because of his condition. I contacted my bank and was told to contact the insurance company, with whom I also insure my car. I submitted a claim for about 900 euros for the refund of flights and the hotel accommodation that had been paid for, and which I assumed were covered by the credit card insurance.

I couldn't have been more wrong. My claim was declined on the grounds that it was my partner who was taken ill and not myself. This was despite the fact that we have a joint credit card on the same account. This seemed a ridiculous situation and I can image many circumstances where flights are booked for husband, wife and possibly children, yet if another member of the party was taken ill there would be no cover. I complained and raised a number of salient points in a letter written in both Spanish and English and sent it to the bank's head office for further consideration, which again was quickly declined.

On this occasion, I had the distinct feeling that because I was an expat living in Spain, I was not being treated in the same way as a Spanish citizen. Discrimination of any kind always makes me angry and so I wrote another, stronger letter in Spanish, threatening to close my bank account, credit card, as well as home and car insurance with the company. I sent this to the bank branch, customer service department, as well as to their Chief Executive at their head office as well as the insurance company. All letters were sent by signed for post, with additional copies sent by fax (which the Spanish still adore) and email, which are usually ignored. It is a process that I call the 'scatter gun' approach to complaints, which usually works for me.

Two days later I received a phone call from the insurance company to tell me that my claim had been reconsidered and that the company had decided to make an ex gratia payment for the full amount. Although it was a victory for me, I would have preferred the payment to be made to me as a matter of right, based upon the conditions of the policy and not simply because I was able to shout loud enough to make a point.

I have learned a lesson; I will no longer trust the free insurance offered with my credit card; indeed, it will be cancelled later in the year and I will be looking for a travel insurance policy with its conditions written clearly in English.

I would be interested to hear from other readers who have had similar claims on their credit card insurance denied, as well as positive experiences with both credit cards and travel insurance. I will place any information about this issue on the expat section of my website, which may be of help to other readers. Meanwhile, when making a complaint against a bank or insurance company in Spain, my advice is never to take no for an answer.

An Island Railway

An island railway has been talked about for many years. Plans have been drawn up, schemes costed by earlier island governments and subsequently cancelled by a later government. However, it now seems that the time has finally come to build a railway in Gran Canaria.

A comparatively small island it may be, yet our main motorway, the GC1, can be a nightmare to travel on. The well trodden route from the airport to the south of the island is a haven for fleets of private ambulances, rushing like vultures to be allowed to take the unfortunate victims from motorway pile-ups to the nearest private hospital, salivating at the thought of additional fees and commissions to be earned from those potentially lucrative travel insurance claims.

Life is certainly unpredictable on this particular stretch of motorway with many vehicle traffic accidents each year, and is one of the reasons why many expats and holidaymakers avoid driving on it, and prefer to travel by bus, which can be a much more tedious option.

Hopefully, all this is about to change with a recent announcement of a feasibility study from the Islands' Ministry of Public Buildings and Works that is responsible for the planning of the new railway in Gran Canaria. A variety of projects will be available to begin from mid 2014, and work could start immediately on the successful bid.

The other good news is that the scheme will create around 18,000 jobs during the first four years of its construction, which would be of huge benefit for an island with around one third of its young labour force currently unemployed. In addition, it will provide additional employment for specialists from Peninsular Spain, as well as from the far reaches of European Union. It is the kind of capital project that the UK Government can only dream about.

It is predicted that the new service will carry around 14.6 million passengers during the first year of operation, which is similar to the current bus service on the island. Journey times of well over an hour from the south of the island to Las Palmas de Gran Canaria, the islands' capital, will be reduced to around 20 minutes, helping both tourists and the business community to make the most of opportunities on the island.

Of course, the usual group of cynics are lining up to veto the project. Bus companies and taxi drivers are, predictably, not too keen on the project. The current PP (right wing) administration is lukewarm on completing the project, since it was introduced by their predecessors, and political games must continue to be played at all costs. Indeed they are already muttering that dreaded word "privatisation," as well as seeking outside contracts with foreign investors. There are those who raise the reasonable point that the 1545 million euros allocated for the project could be spent on many other things, forgetting that the funds are earmarked for this project alone from outside sources and cannot be spent on other things, as desirable as it may be. Failure to complete the project would result in not only the loss of funding, but the 18 to 24 million euros already spent at the planning stage would also be wasted.

Opponents sharing similar views to those of the Daily Hate in the UK are horrified at the thought of more wind turbines on the island, which will generate all the power necessary to power the railway, plus additional capacity, which will help to reduce the islands' growing dependence upon oil. Environmentalists complain about destruction and disturbances during the building of the track, conveniently overlooking the fact that much of the project will be underground in order to overcome most of the environmental issues. Residents and tourists only have to drive through the new tunnel to Puerto Mogan in the south of the island to realise that island engineers are rather good at cutting though mountains nowadays, leaving minimal damage upon completion.

Personally, I cannot wait for the day that the new island railway is open and I have my fingers crossed that a station will not be too far from my home. Anything to reduce congestion and accidents on the dreaded GC1 would be of great benefit to tourists and residents alike, but I remain doubtful that an opening date of 2018 for the new service will actually happen.

Local Culture and Diversity

Some People are Gay - Get Over it!

Gay Pride is always a magnificent spectacle and a huge party in Gran Canaria, and preparations are well underway for this year's spectacular. After all, Maspalomas Pride is one of the biggest events of its kind in the world. The very first Gay Pride in Maspalomas took place in May 2001, and we have seen the festival become more impressive each year. Thousands of gay men and women, as well as transgendered and bisexual people (LGBT), from across the world visit the island to have fun in the sun, as well as to enjoy the shows and street parade of the big weekend. This year's Pride will be a time of parties, cultural events and shows. Those tourists and residents who are new to the island, as well as readers of 'Twitters from the Atlantic' may well be asking themselves, "What is all the fuss about?"

The first ever Gay Pride parade took place in 1969 and is known as the March on Stonewall. The event started as a protest against discrimination and violence against gay men and women in New York City. Although there have been many advances in equality since those dark days, it is time once again to ask ourselves if anything has really changed, or is it mostly superficial?

Each day we still read and hear of gay men and women who are persecuted for their sexuality. In some countries, gay men and women are still strung up and publicly hanged from cranes as a warning to others. In other countries, the mind games that are played are subtler, but still have the same devastating effect upon men and women who have committed no crime, other than a desire to love and be loved.

History has taught us that during times of financial hardship, poverty and recession, it is always the minority groups who are oppressed. We saw this at its most horrific in Nazi Germany with the persecution of Jews, gypsies, disabled children and gay men and women, where a trip to the gas chambers was seen as "the final solution".

Have we really learned anything? We are already seeing some repetition of hate crimes towards gay men and women, and others who are not considered as "normal" by the wider population. A recent appalling article in the Daily Mail, known by many as the Daily Fascist or the Daily Hate, written by the columnist Littlejohn, wrote an obnoxious article about a primary school teacher undergoing a sex change operation that was widely reported as having led to her recent suicide. We know that verbal "gay bashing" is the order of the day for some unholy alliances of churches with doctrines as far apart as Catholics, Muslims and the Mormons. Right wing political parties continue to spread their message of hate in the UK, Spain, France and the US, and polls reveal that these parties are gaining in popularity as a result.

Recent debates about gay marriage in the UK, US, Spain and France have revealed many long held and carefully hidden prejudices that have shaken many gay men and women out of their relative complacency of hard won battles over the generations. The gay marriage issue has made many gay men and women realise that their 'acceptance' is only surface deep, and the hatred and disgust shown by many who deny gay men and women the right to love members of their own gender leave us in no doubt that gay equality does not and has never truly existed.

Maybe we have been lulled into a kind of security by crumbs thrown from the political table in the guise of civil partnerships and laws attempting to protect. However, although there have undoubtedly been many improvements in the lives of gay men and women, the attitudes of many remain unchanged, and hypocrisy still continues as recent debates surrounding gay marriage reveal.

Today, Gay Pride events have become an annual ritual all over the world and have grown to include thousands of gay and gay-friendly participants, families and friends of gay, lesbian, transgender and bisexual people, as well as hundreds of spectators. We look forward to and will enjoy Maspalomas Gay Pride as usual; let us all enjoy a well-earned party of celebration. However, we should never forget the hard won fight of those who have gone before us. Let us remain on our guard, and continue to be aware of the on going challenges.

'Wall to Wall Homosexuals'

As a columnist, I expect to receive a spot of criticism from time to time. Although it is good to receive praise and favourable comments from readers, this is unlikely to happen all the time. We all have our own points of view and, thank goodness, we live in a part of the world that still allows freedom of expression. I hope that I can express views and ideas in a way that is enjoyable and amusing, but also in a way that is sometimes intended to extend ideas and to challenge conventional thinking.

In the run up to Maspalomas Gay Pride in Gran Canaria, which is one of the largest in Europe and lasts for well over one hectic, but most enjoyable week, I wrote an article called 'Some People Are Gay, Get Over It'. Sadly, poor Colin, one of my readers, is currently skulking in the mountains to escape "Wall to Wall Homosexuals", as he put it. He did not get over it, and wrote me a most unpleasant, yet very sad, email. Although I will not reproduce the message in full here, as it is offensive, Colin criticised gay men and women for not being sensitive to the views of "normal" people" (I still have to find some of those), and finds the idea of "two men (or women) having a physical and sexual relationship both repulsive and disgusting". It was sad to read that Colin and his wife fled "this hotbed of evil" to escape to the mountains, where they would find "peace, tranquillity, and no raging homosexuals kissing and cuddling". However, they will no doubt be shocked to discover that they are now surrounded by some rather randy goats.

Well, there we have it. I was certainly put in my place and although I try to respect everyone's opinions, I would have respected Colin's opinion even more if he had given me the right of reply. Yes, you guessed it, his email address was of course not in use and I doubt that Colin is his real name anyway, although from what I hear from other readers, Colin has already been identified; after all, it is a small island.

I am not about to repeat the reasons here why we defend the rights of gay men and women to be themselves in an outward demonstration of solidarity during Gay Pride. Others have already done this, very successfully, many times, and in many different ways over the years. However, what I will say quite simply to Colin and others like him is that no one has a monopoly on love, nor do they have the right to choose whom we love.

Several people have complained to me over the last few days about the disruption, noise and inconvenience that Gay Pride brings to the island each year. They may choose to forget the huge amount of money from tourism that this spectacular event brings to the islands' economy each year, during what used to be 'the quiet season'. Not any more; additional flights, full bars, restaurants and hotels all greatly benefit from the huge increase in business, which many survive on for the remainder of the year. For most, it is time for a great party and a huge celebration of what has been achieved by gay men and women over the years.

Gay Pride is not all about business, making money and dressing up for the occasion; it is much more serious and challenging than this. It is a time when we can remember those who have fought for equality, and remind others and ourselves that gay men and women across the world still struggle in their daily lives. To those that say the battle has been won, and we should no longer have Gay Pride and Gay Parades, they have only to read the newspapers and watch television to realise that we do not have true equality. The vicious and on-going debate about gay marriage, the torture and execution of gay men and women across the world are just two examples of struggles that continue.

Then there is Colin, who is still skulking in the mountains and complaining about "Wall to Wall Homosexuals" at every opportunity. Well, as this wonderful island is already highly inclusive, with a strong 'live and let live' attitude, I suspect that Colin may well now be in the minority this week. I am sorry that my 'Some People are Gay, Get Over It' article offended Colin and others like him, but he should be aware that some people are straight, and we have had to get over it.

Rocking the Boats

Hatred, rivalries and jealousies are a feature of human nature that, sadly, can continue for many years. If left unresolved, they become poisonous and destructive with implications that spread far beyond the original squabble. Such rivalries apply to families, countries and even to islands.

For most people, these seven islands in the Atlantic are a haven of peace and tranquillity. There is an illusion that these islands cooperate and work well together as an autonomous community within Spain. The islands benefit from a shared history, culture, mutual understanding, a shared dependency and have common concerns about the economy, unemployment, health and environmental issues, such as exploration for oil off the coast of Africa. However, is this glossy facade really true?

Needless to say, much of this cooperation is really only skin deep. Bitter rivalries between the islands and, in particular, between Gran Canaria and Tenerife have existed for many hundreds of years, peaking during the horrors of the Spanish Civil War. Nowadays, we have only to attend a football match or other major sporting event between the two rivals to witness current manifestations of unresolved bitterness, jealousy and rivalry. Just add a dose of Spanish machismo on a very hot day, and you can imagine the result.

Although Tenerife is the largest island, with the largest population of all the islands, the city of Las Palmas in Gran Canaria is the largest city on any of the islands. Indeed, Las Palmas de Gran Canaria is the seventh largest city in all of Spain. In addition, the airport of Gran Canaria dwarfs those on Tenerife, with its large number of national and international flights, as well as being the third largest airport in Spain. Tenerife and Gran Canaria have squabbled ferociously in the past as to which city should be regarded as the capital city of the Canary Islands, Santa Cruz de Tenerife or Las Palmas de Gran Canaria? The outcome was, of course, the usual compromise that they should both hold equal status. There was much anguish about where the islands' prestigious universities and hospitals should be situated. The answer was to duplicate everything for the benefit of both islands. There is, of course, always a Canarian compromise, but only after much macho shouting, unpronounceable expletives and table banging. It's just the way that things are done over here.

The current spat between the Mayors of Santa Cruz de Tenerife and Las Palmas de Gran Canaria is another fine example of such a squabble. Las Palmas recently accused Tenerife of 'cooking the books', with its inclusion of over 13,000 "ghost residents" in its statistical submission designed, naturally enough, to enhance its quota of funding from the Government. By now we all know that statistics can be interpreted and distorted by politicians to mean anything. Predictably, the Mayor of Tenerife and the President of the Tenerife Cabildo are now accusing the Mayor of Las Palmas of similar evil doings with dark suggestions that they too "may be surprised" if they examine their own statistics too closely. Despite the squabble, and much huffing and puffing, they will eventually kiss and make up - until the next time, that is.

Of course, there is a small independence movement on the islands, which makes impressive and strident claims during local and national elections that the Canary Islands would benefit from being an independent state, completely divorced from Spain. After all, the Scots are trying to do it, so why not the Canary Islands? It is, of course, great rhetoric, but totally ignores the reality that the islands just do not get on with each other, and that they need Spain to keep them from capsizing each other's metaphorical boat.

The arguments and accusations go on, and will continue just as they have always done. After all, it is much like the love-hate relationship between Britain and France. They may dislike each other intensely, but support each other when the going gets tough.

Just One More Flush

Do please make sure that you have consumed your breakfast and been to the bathroom before reading this Twitter, as its contents may upset the delicate (as well as those affected by strobe lighting)...

There is a sewage pumping station in our village and, from time to time, council workers in spaceman suits and helmets, thick rubber gloves and masks appear to de-clog it, wash it, change filters or do whatever one does to a sewage pump. Without going into too much detail, the stench is horrendous and if anyone happens to want to drop their rubbish bag into the adjacent skip, the task is best completed by holding one's breath, placing a handkerchief over the nose and mouth and completing the job as quickly as possible.

It was one of those beautiful sunny mornings when I happened to arrive at the rubbish skip at the same time as the sewage workers. After I had dropped my bag of rubbish into the skip and dashed away in an attempt to reach unpolluted air, to my horror I noticed that one of the workers had not only a jet wash pipe in one hand, but a large sandwich in the other ungloved hand. He was clearly enjoying his crusty mid-morning breakfast, and I guess the man should be applauded for working at the same time as eating. However, my stomach did a double somersault before I headed for home and a gargle of whisky, which I am convinced kills all known germs and is far more effective than antibiotics.

I tried to convince myself that probably a few germs are actually quite good for all of us in this sanitised world, before my mind moved on to another associated issue. Did you realise that the authorities are now testing sewage for illicit drugs? You see, although it is quite easy to outwit the system when being questioned or completing a survey for the authorities, toilet contents simply don't lie. Indeed, to their credit, urine and poo are blisteringly truthful. It is the new science of sewer epidemiology, which is currently used in many European cities to test for the usage of illicit drugs. Indeed, at the whisk of a test tube, it is now possible to test a city, part of a city or single street to reveal which naughty people have been snorting coke, using weed or worse.

Sewers simply reek with honesty. After all, in most developed countries, every household has a toilet, which is connected to the central sewage system, and everyone goes to the toilet from time-to-time. Forget surveys and questionnaires, the exact quantities of drug consumption are clearly available for all to see by using this method. These tests simply go into overdrive when testing for cannabis, cocaine and ecstasy. Interestingly, but not surprisingly, the statistics skyrocket during the Christmas and the New Year festivities, yet it is worrying that people also appear to take similar amounts of cannabis during workdays as holidays. Just bear that one in mind when you next see your dentist. That shaky hand holding the threatening drill head, which you had previously dismissed as stress or simply getting old, may indicate that he is stoned. The toilet test will reveal all such secrets.

In the US, this exciting new development is now widely used to give police better intelligence, as well as helping hospitals to anticipate demand for their drug rehabilitation services. The system is also being used to help to identify illicit new drugs, helping police with law enforcement priorities, as well as allowing hospitals and public health authorities to warn users about the risks of taking drugs. Bad drugs can also be identified, allowing public warning notices to be issued.

Despite the wonders of this new technology, I do feel some unease. Is nothing sacred and private anymore? We already have snoopers listening into our mobile phone calls, accessing our emails and text messages, and now they are examining the contents of our toilets. I strongly suspect that there is far more that the authorities are not telling us and I am convinced that Big Brother already knows that Barrie Mahoney polished off half a bottle of decent Rioja with his evening meal, and finished it off with a large brandy. After all, sewage doesn't lie.

The Guagua

My grandfather was a carrier, which is a term that is not in common use nowadays. When he started his business, he owned a horse-drawn bus, which he used to transport people and produce from village to village or town. It became a very popular service, and I remember as a child that my grandfather was always referred to with great affection in the area long after he had died. As well as owning a bus, he also had a great love of pocket watches, which for him was a relatively modern technology, and of course helped to provide local people with a very reliable service in all kinds of weather.

Later, my grandfather upgraded from horses to motorised buses, and was the first carrier in Lincolnshire to own and run his own motorised bus. He operated a regular service to several destinations, such as the town of Boston on market days, and bracing Skegness for a spot of sea air at the weekends. He increased his ownership of these mechanised marvels, until his small fleet was eventually taken over by a much larger organisation that had set up in competition. Grandad's motorised buses were seen as a modern marvel in the area, but I also remember being horrified when I learned as a child that both my mother and aunt, who had never taken or passed a driving test in their lives, were regularly recruited as relief bus drivers and, by all accounts, my Aunt was particularly good at it. Thankfully, they both gave up the job before too many other vehicles took to the road.

Travelling by bus is a relatively new discovery for me. Until recently, I have rarely set foot on a bus, but travelling to Las Palmas by car is no longer a pleasant option unless I really know where I am going to park, because car parking is difficult to find, as well as very expensive. Expats living on the island often forget that Las Palmas de Gran Canaria is the seventh largest city in Spain, which probably explains why it usually reminds me of driving a car in central London, but without the congestion zone charges.

Now that I have understood the timetable for buses on the island, I find that travelling to the city is a relatively cheap and reliable option. One must also be a little flexible and allow for 'Canarian time', which is never taken too seriously over here. A bus will usually turn up eventually, even if not exactly to schedule. On the other hand, I have found most drivers to be polite and helpful, and most are willing to give advice about times and the best bus to travel on for a particular destination. Travelling by bus is also great fun for people watching, which is one of my favourite pastimes. We only have to travel from Las Palmas to the south of the island late on a Saturday night or in early hours of Sunday morning, to realise that just as we are going home to bed, most young Canarians are on their way out for the night in the south. If you like people watching, I can thoroughly recommend it as a source of endless entertainment and amusement. Indeed, I am quite sure that some of the more colourful characters observed recently will appear in future books.

The word, 'guagua' has a fascinating history, since it comes from the days when British businessmen in Las Palmas used wagons to transport people, produce and materials around the island. The word 'wagon' was painted on the sides and back of these vehicles. 'Guagua', is the term used in the Canary Islands for the word 'bus'. It is a lovely word to say, and if you say the word 'wagon' with a Canarian accent, you will hear what I mean! Canarians have a different pronunciation of the 'w' sound and therefore the term 'wagon' became corrupted to the rather charming word 'guagua', which has remained in use on the islands to this day. Although used in South America, 'guagua' is not a word often heard in Peninsular Spain, where 'autobus' is the usual term. Initially horses or camels drew these wagons or guaguas on the Canary Islands, but later these were mechanised, just like my grandfather's bus.

Treasure Island

I have always been fascinated with the idea of living on an island. As a child, I always knew that I would live on an island one day, although I thought it may be the Isle of Wight, the Isles of Scilly or even the Isle of Islay, off Scotland's magnificent west coast. The Isle of Islay was a close shave, because I once spotted the perfect croft very close to my favourite malt whisky distillery. However, it does tend to be a rather damp and forbidding place for much of the year, but I will save that story for another time...

Traditionally and politically, the Canary Islands consist of seven main populated islands of Gran Canaria, Tenerife, Lanzarote, Fuerteventura, La Palma, La Gomera and El Hierro. There are also other inhabited, as well as uninhabited islets, known as the Chinijo Archipelago. These include: La Graciosa, Alegranza, Montaña Clara, Roque del Oeste, Roque de Este and Los Lobos. Each island is unique and offers something for everyone. The smaller islands provide greater privacy and a quieter atmosphere than their larger and busier counterparts.

Currently, the 600-strong population of the Island of Graciosa, which is Spanish for funny or amusing, are hoping to become recognised as the eighth Canary Island. Islanders have already collected 4,000 signatures for a campaign that they hope will bring greater autonomy to the 29-square-kilometre island. It is the third smallest island in the archipelago; the island of La Graciosa has two piers and a dock for yachts in the bay, yet no tarmac roads. However, it is currently heavily dependent upon its big sister island, Lanzarote, for most of its supplies and services.

Islanders are claiming that the Canary Islands Regional Government is incorrect in classifying La Graciosa as an isle, as this term is used to define a small island with no population. The islanders point out that, to the contrary, La Graciosa is populated, and to further strengthen their case, the islanders comment that around 25,000 visitors significantly enhance their numbers each year. It seems that the islanders crave for the opportunity to manage their own day-to-day affairs, and not to turn to their larger sister island, Lanzarote, for services such as rubbish collection, or whenever there are interruptions in the island's electricity and water supplies.

At this stage, however, the islanders are not looking to set up their own island council, as with the other seven Canary Islands, but to become recognised as a district, generating and attracting its own funding and without the need for financial hand outs from the Canary Islands Government.

This island is visited by many who wish to escape the busier islands, and to bask in its natural beauty and unspoilt beaches. It is a paradise for those interested in bird watching of the feathered variety, hiking, mountain biking, surfing and kite surfing. Now, I do not wish to be held responsible for encouraging a sudden influx of lobster coloured tourists to this beautiful unspoilt Canary island, islet or isle, in search of yet another pina colada, but I will merely add that this jewel in the Canary Islands' crown is reputed to be the island where Robert Louis Stevenson set his classic novel, Treasure Island.

Throwing knives at Mother

No, rest assured, this is not another harrowing tale of domestic violence, but a skilful performance by Dorian Ledda and his family who have been performing in Gran Canaria's Sioux City for the last 28 years or so...

These were the opening words of an article that I wrote for a magazine several years ago, following a visit to Sioux City, which could best be described as a Wild West experience on an island in the Atlantic. It is the stuff that generations of boys and girls read about in their comic books and watched countless films of baddies being dealt instant justice by goodies. Sadly, Sioux City is no more, as it closed its gates for the last time a few days ago, for financial reasons, after 42 years of faithful service to the cowboy loving public on holiday in our island paradise.

The Cañon del Aguila (Eagle Canyon) offered a barren landscape and gave the perfect opportunity to recreate a pioneer Old West town based in the 1850s, with real buildings that are unique in Europe with a complete construction, and not just simple film set frontages. Sioux City was just the stuff to feed the imagination, relive childhood memories, as well as being a great place for a day out.

The town was constructed and used as a film set in 1972, at a cost of two million dollars, for major Hollywood Wild West films, such as Clint Eastwood's 'A Fistful of Dollars', 'A Few Dollars More' and 'Take a Long Hard Ride'. Gran Canaria's desert-like landscape in the south of the island was just right for this kind of film in those days.

Once filmmaking was completed, the set became redundant and was opened to the public as a theme park with a difference. Until last week, visitors would wander expectantly through the gates of this Wild West town and be instantly transported into a world of cowboys and Indians, bar brawls and bank hold-ups.

It is in this Wild West town that I interviewed Dorian Ledda and his family – mother, Katy and brothers Davide and Daniele, an Italian family from Turin, who presented breathtaking performances of knife throwing, lassoes, whips and horse riding. Originally the Ledda family performed in Italian circuses, theatres and television before moving to Gran Canaria thirty years ago.

Dorian's father was throwing knives at his mother when she was pregnant with Dorian, and so throwing knives at mother seemed the most natural thing in the world to do!

Dorian's brother, Daniele, also featured in the Guinness World Book of Records for jumping with a lasso, as well as appearing in a feature for the BBC. Dorian and his two brothers performed at Sioux City and Katy had knives, axes and flaming torches thrown at her.

Indeed, watching the poor lady endure this torment from her sons with such a contented smile on her face made for a very unusual Sunday morning's entertainment!

Although the knife throwing act was performed several times a day for the last thirty years, fortunately without an accident, I couldn't help thinking that it would not be a good idea to have a row with your sons or let them throw knives at you after a night of partying!

Sadly, this fictional universe and unique recreational activity for tourists visiting the island, created as a labour of love by several generations of craftsmen and entertainers over four decades, has now come to an end. Like so many who know Sioux City well, I hope that a way will be found to open it once again to an adoring public, who can once again watch magnificent horses, can-can dancers in beautiful frilly costumes, cowboys falling from buildings, as well as Indians throwing knives at mother…

Los Miserables in the Canary Islands

It has been a long time since I have been to the cinema, maybe ten years or so. It's not that I don't like movies; it is that I much prefer to see a live show or concert, or watching movies at home. Indeed, one of the things that I do miss as an expat, alongside Marmite and mince pies, is the occasional visit to London's West End or a Madrid theatre to see the latest play or musical. One of my all time favourites is Les Miserables, which I think I have now seen seven times, and never tire of its moving plot and exhilarating, spiritual music.

The only exception to this acute neglect of the cinematic experience was a one-time visit to an open-air cinema. It was a bit of a novelty, and fascinating experience to watch a movie beneath a starlit sky on a warm summer's evening, but not one that I would care to repeat. I, like many others, found that mosquitoes and other flying insects feasting and attacking our skin tended to lead to a lack of concentration on the film.

So, after ten years, in was off to our local multiplex, to see Los Miserables. The cinema seemed to be mainly focussed upon selling huge buckets of popcorn, pick and mix sweets - Woolworth's style, as well as huge quantities of over priced fizzy drinks. I shuddered to think of the calorific and caffeine content included in these treats, but recognise that it is all part of the modern cinematic experience and, I guess, forms a substantial and welcome part of the overall takings.

The cinema showing our film was small, yet very comfortable, and I was very impressed with the comfort of the armchair style seats - much improved since the last time I visited any cinema. There were the usual run of trailers advertising future films, but sadly no 'Pearl and Dean' advertising or a pre-feature film! Yes, those days have long gone, as have those smartly dressed ladies bearing a tray full of frozen goodies at half time. What did surprise me, in this age of 3D, Dolby, surround and stereo sound, was the appalling quality of sound during this film. The sound appeared to be coming from a couple of speakers directly beneath the screen, with no surround or stereo sound in existence. Maybe the right knobs on the control panel hadn't been adjusted correctly, and I was itching to help the projectionist to sort out the problem with his woofers and tweeters. Sadly, there was no one in sight to ask, and I guess that the controls for the film were pre-set and being operated from a remote control centre somewhere in Madrid. We get far better sound quality from our basic home cinema system.

However, a range of interesting sounds from the bucket popcorn and nachos chompers were received in full stereo sound, as were the anticipated coughs and sniffs during the emotional scenes of the film. I was surprised that very young children were also in the audience, including one group of seven-year-olds, complete with balloons and hats, who seemed to arrive from a children's birthday party. The children were mostly very well behaved, although both the Brit and teacher in me felt distinctly uncomfortable when I realised that they too were witnessing the unpleasant, yet brief, prostitute/rape scene. Clearly, there are no British Board of Film Censor categories and prohibitions over here.

It was an experience. The film was good, but I think I would be adding, "Could do better" on the end of term report card for the cinema. As for those cynics who said that making a film would put people off from seeing the stage show. Certainly not. I know which version I much prefer and I will be heading to London's West End for a refresher the next time that I am in the UK.

A Home in the Sun

Recently billed as a "storm raging" about "the shocking", but some would say accurate, portrayal of the seedier side of life in Gran Canaria, gave quite a few of us a good laugh recently. Indignation and denial from the tourist board was the immediate reaction to the recent Spanish television programme broadcast, which was, according to the programme makers, intended to give an honest portrayal of the places that it visits - warts and all. However, I suspect that sensationalism rather than honesty was the most important thing on the producer's mind during filming.

From sordid accounts of sex workers plying their trade to tourists, to swingers, drugs and rum drinking youngsters intent on forcing their charms on unsuspecting tourists reminded me of similar antics reportedly taking place in Ibiza and Majorca, as well as Blackpool, Brighton and Rhyl. Well, it is all the stuff of good, seedy, summer television isn't it?

Gran Canaria is a very popular holiday destination that appeals to many different age and interest groups. The island's long established 'live and let live' attitude is one of the key factors in this island paradise that appeals to so many, and is the reason why many moved to this island. As long as it doesn't hurt anyone else, anything goes, within reason, of course. Naturally, this view of life irritates and shocks some people, but I suspect that it titivates more than it offends the majority. There are few cities in Europe, including the UK, that doesn't have sex workers, legal or otherwise; indeed, I suspect that a city that is drug, alcohol and swinger free is unique in Europe.

The tourist board of Gran Canaria, as well as some of its citizens, are said to be shocked by the recent revelations, fearing that the negative publicity will undermine the recent hard work that has gone into promoting the island as an international tourist destination. As a firm believer in the saying that there is no such thing as bad publicity, I suspect that after a little fuss and hot air being blown by local politicians and priests, they have nothing to worry about in the long term.

On a more serious note, I recently received a request from a 'television company' asking me to participate in their offering for would be expats. Most readers will remember good quality programmes, such as "A Place in the Sun" aimed at helping would be expats to fulfil their dreams of expat life. However, an endless and tedious succession of dubious 'copycat' programmes such as "Overseas Builders from Hell" and "Overseas Homes from Hell", which delighted in poking fun, publicising and exaggerating the demise of the expat who actually had the courage to fulfil a long held desire and dream of moving to another country. Of course, such programmes often fulfil that well-known and unfortunate British trait of knocking the successful, as well as the envy and jealousy of those who have something that they do not.

Such programmes are rarely worthy of airtime, and are usually low budget affairs made by one-off television companies established specifically for the purpose. Although they are often promoted under the respectable guise of BBC, ITV, Channel 4 etc, in reality they are nothing of the kind. The programme's 'researchers' usually do little more than contact local publications and businesses in their target area, asking for a list of likely people who would be willing to contribute to their programme. Most people are initially flattered by the request and will happily participate in such programmes, only to be embarrassed by the time that the programme is aired. I know several people who have contributed to such programmes, and who have later been horrified by the way that their contribution has been edited, or simply ignored, because it failed the sensationalism test that was considered essential to give the negative spin that the programme makers desired.

In my own case, careful questioning of the researcher, as well as the programme's producer, revealed that they were looking to sensationalise the negative aspects of moving abroad, with a focus upon the possibility of losing everything should the euro collapse, yet another slant on the 'land grab' situation in Spain, as well as the collapse of the Spanish building industry. Needless to say, I declined their offer.

So if you are an expat in Spain, do be wary if you receive a phone call from someone in the UK who begins the conversation with "I'm from the

BBC/ITV/Sky etc." On a cold, wet, winter's evening in the UK, I firmly believe that most people prefer a good news story, as well as something to feed their hopes and dreams of a life in the sun.

Expat Dilemmas and Considerations

The
Canary
Islander

Stuck in a lift

I developed an intense dislike of lifts after being stuck in one with my brother, sister-in-law and nephew one afternoon a few years ago. I have also recently witnessed two engineers attempting to repair a lift in one of the commercial centres with a pair of scissors, a strip of corrugated card and a tube of super glue. Now, I am not an engineer, but I strongly suspect that this procedure may not lead to the most effective lift repair. No, as far as I am concerned, it is far better to use the stairs. It is good exercise and one usually lives longer.

I recently had to visit a nearby empty apartment for a friend in the UK who was trying desperately trying to sell his apartment in the Canary Islands. It was an apartment on the fifth floor of a very smart, but empty building. After looking suspiciously at the metal lift doors, which were already pitted with rust, I headed for the dusty staircase. The apartment had only been used for a few short holidays, and was part of a block of apartments where building had ground to a halt at the start of the recession, and after the builders had gone into liquidation. My friend had finally found someone who was very interested in purchasing it, albeit at a knock down price, and he asked if I would mind giving it a "pre-inspection once over", and giving the floors a quick mop.

After two tiring hours of energetically cleaning floors and windows I was tired, and decided to risk taking the lift to the ground floor. I was initially reassured by the smooth opening of the lift doors, as I clambered inside with my mop and bucket, and pressed the button with confidence. Two seconds after starting my descent, there was a loud grating noise and the lift shuddered to an undignified halt. I pressed the door-opening button and nothing happened. I pressed the alarm button, but there was no sound. Panicking slightly, I pressed the intercom button; predictably, there was no response. I attempted to force the door open with my hands, but there was no movement whatsoever. A feeling of déjà vu suddenly swept over me.

Repeated attempts at button pressing, trying to force the doors open, and even jumping up and down had no effect, other than raising my blood pressure. It was now getting very warm inside the lift, and I remembered that too much exertion would reduce oxygen levels more quickly than if I remained calm and inactive. It was then that I remembered that there was no one else living on the top floor of the apartment block, other than an elderly lady who was visiting her niece in the UK, and a young couple and a baby living on the ground floor. There really was no reason for anyone to take the lift to the top floor.

I tried to use my mobile phone but, of course, there was no signal. Well, at least I still had light, or was that disappearing too? Maybe I was imagining that it was dimming slightly. It looked as if I was in for the long haul. Maybe I would be in there until my skeletonised remains were discovered one day in the future, still clutching a bucket and mop. I just wished

I was wearing smarter clothes, and not my old baggy jeans and a grubby sweatshirt. I had heard that expiring through a lack of oxygen is not a particularly pleasant way to die, but there are worse ways, such as plunging into a lift shaft or getting limbs caught up in the lift mechanism. I shuddered at the thought. The future suddenly looked very bleak indeed.

As a cub scout, albeit briefly, I was taught always to be prepared, which made far more sense than all that "dib, dibbing" nonsense that was a ritual, and much loved by scout leaders at that time. As a result, I had a tough old penknife and bottle opener in my bag, although I remember wondering as a seven-year-old, why a bottle opener was so important in dealing with emergencies, but I later learned that my scoutmaster was an alcoholic, which could have explained its inclusion. Using the bottle opener, I managed to force a gap between the doors, which was just sufficient to force in the broom handle. One hefty yank later, and the handle of the broom split, and then the lift doors creaked open to reveal daylight!

The lift rested between two floors, so I had the choice of two methods of escape. I reasoned that it would be better to climb upwards and then squeeze onto the floor above, rather than to crawl through a smaller gap in the door and fall onto whatever lay below. I finally appeared as an exhausted heap on the second floor, firmly resolving to walk, or use an escalator in future.

Flushed with Success

Regular 'Twitters from the Atlantic' readers will no doubt be delighted and will celebrate with me in knowing that Venezuela's National Assembly has at last backed plans to import 39 million rolls of toilet paper, in an effort to relieve a chronic shortage, indeed a blockage, of this essential household item, which we all take for granted.

Although Venezuela is rich in oil, it relies heavily on imports, but currency controls have affected its ability to pay for foreign imports. Sadly, toilet rolls are currently in very short supply in Venezuelan shops, and I understand that they are almost impossible to purchase, other than on the black market, where the quality is variable. However, the new President, Nicolas Maduro, who won a narrow majority in April's Presidential elections, has come to the rescue, although he blames the country's shortage of toilet paper upon a conspiracy by the opposition and rich and evil members of society, who have bought up the country's annual allowance at a knock down price, resulting in a phenomena, which is commonly and crudely termed by economists as 'bog roll inflation.'

Although we are currently witnessing violent protests concerning the recession and Spanish football teams, just imagine the chaos and resulting anarchy if we popped into our local supermarket for a few rolls of supersoft, only to be told that the opposition was cruelly withholding all supplies. I suspect that would be the time that most expats would be putting any available copies of the Daily Hate to its proper and intended use. Maybe tabloids come in useful after all?

All this excitement about toilet rolls has reminded me that the sewage pumping station in our village has finally given up the ghost, or should I say, ended its triumphant mashing days in the village pumping station. Some villagers have cruelly suggested that the narrowness of pipework leading to the pumping station, in an effort by builders to reduce costs, has contributed to the problem, whilst others suggest that the existing pump is just not able to cope with all the local effluent, as well as excessively thick toilet paper. No doubt, this issue will be debated for years to come.

For many days now, there have been anxious faces in overalls, accompanied by anxious faces in suits, peering into a newly dug hole adjacent to the very smart, newly painted building, that houses this precious, but grossly under valued machinery. There has been much shaking of hands, and exasperated gesturing of hands before anyone has so much as picked up a screwdriver. Local residents have been seriously concerned that a trip to the loo was about to mean a drive to an adjacent town, should the village flush fail to function.

All is not lost. I am pleased to report that a new and much larger engine has been shipped from Peninsular Spain, at great expense, and just been installed. However, disappointingly, it continues to be accompanied by much shaking of heads and dramatic hand gesturing by both overalls and suits alike. However, to the great relief of villagers, I can report that all flushing functions remain on line and fully active.

Meanwhile, I am sure that I speak for many in celebrating the fact that Venezuela now has its own supply of toilet rolls, although I cannot speak for the operation of its pumping stations, which I understand are few and far between. Despite the comments from unkind cynics, I suggest that this should be celebrated as a real triumph of democracy, as politicians are at last listening to and meeting the true needs of its people. Meanwhile, may I suggest the greater use of the dreaded bidet, or supplying Izal, which under no circumstances could be described as 'a soft tissue', to reduce excessive consumption? I guess they are just longing to see the Andrex puppy advert on TV!

Eyes Down for Harmless Expat Fun

Many expats move to their new home in the sun without being fully aware of national and local laws, together with the consequences if they fail to abide by them. When we moved to Spain, we were often told by more experienced expats to be very careful on the roads just before Christmas and not to upset the police. Rumour had it that the police were unnecessarily harsh during such periods, and would take every opportunity to fine wrong doers. This, it was said, was to pay for their bonus and Christmas parties. I doubted that this was true, but I did notice a startling correlation at the time. However, whatever the truth, it is true that many expats take the view of "ignore it and it will go away." Sadly, ignorance of the law is no defence in any circumstances, and the wise expat needs to be aware of this fact.

Brits are generally very fond of a bit of bingo, particularly if they are expats living in the sun, or are on holiday. Bingo is as British as fish and chips, a pint of "best" and wearing a knotted handkerchief on holiday. I don't remember playing the game for many years, but I do remember it as a bit of harmless fun, and from which a lot of people get much pleasure. I recall many expat bars in Spain's Costa Blanca and Costa del Sol, where bingo evenings (and afternoons) are highly popular events, providing a welcome stream of regulars to otherwise empty bars, as well as a providing a valuable source of fund raising revenue for many local charities who would benefit from the proceeds. It also provided a regular social event and company for those expats who had moved abroad and were anxious to make friends with like-minded people in their neighbourhood.

Did I say harmless fun? This is where the cynic would say that this is the cue for someone to step in and stop it. Well, this is just what happened to the owner of an expat bar in Portugal's Algarve not so long ago.

It was one of those Friday night events when a well meaning landlady, let us call her Dot, decided to raise a few euros by providing a little entertainment for her regulars. A tin of biscuits, a large bar of chocolate and a few cheap drinks were the prizes on offer - hardly the stuff of the Las Vegas gambling scene, but sufficient to tempt 28 of her regulars into the bar for a few drinks and a game of bingo in good company.

It all seemed to be going well as the regulars settled down for a few games. However, shortly after starting the game, a number of armed police burst into the bar and, having checked out the situation during several earlier Friday evening visits in plain clothes, decided to put an end to all to this decadence and villainy by raiding the bar, and arresting Dot and her punters. Before the enthusiastic bingo players could even call "House", Dot and her 28 regulars were bundled into police vans and driven off to the cells, accused of attending an illegal gambling den. Even the prizes, a tin of biscuits, a large bar of chocolate and some drinks, were impounded as "evidence" to be placed before the magistrate.

Later, Dot was charged, appeared before the magistrate and fined 700 euros, as well as receiving a suspended four-month prison sentence. Dot's regulars were a little more fortunate and were charged with "exploitation of illegal gambling, illegal gambling and witnessing illegal gambling" and fined 150 euros each.

The Portuguese police responded to enquiries from the press by commenting that the raid had been carried out following "information reported by anonymous citizens". Hmm, I may be jumping to conclusions, but by that I assume that a nearby bar owner, jealous of Dot's successful business strategy, had reported her to his friends at the police station. Portugal it seems has strict controls on such expat fun, and premises have to apply for a gambling licence, which Dot was clearly unaware of.

So what happened to the prizes? I understand that the police returned the tin of biscuits and alcohol to Dot, but I do wonder what happened to the chocolate? As for Dot? Well, she has decided never to play a game of bingo again.

Are your savings safe?

Many expats moved to Spain and the Canary Islands at a time when borrowing money from Spanish banks was a relatively simple and straightforward affair. Obtaining a mortgage in Spain, often through the developers of new build properties, and usually at a very good rate of interest, was something that many expats took advantage of. In addition, credit cards, often with very high credit limits, suddenly became freely available in Spain. Unlike the UK, the credit card phenomenon was a relatively new innovation in Spain, but was an opportunity grasped with enthusiasm by both Spanish and expats alike.

As we all know, it is now payback time. Funds are no longer as freely available as they once were and Spanish banks continue to tighten their rules, often without notifying their customers. One of the consequences of this new fiscal tightening has been the impact upon credit cards issued by banks. Previously, as in the UK, credit cards in Spain were issued on the basis of a credit check, as well as checking the customer's account history. However, from a number of emails that I have received recently, it appears that a new dimension has been added to guarantee that the debt will eventually be repaid to the bank.

It appears that many Spanish banks now link credit cards issued to any deposits that are made with the bank by their customers. For those who are fortunate enough to have savings this will have little effect, until they attempt to withdraw their savings. It seems that such customers will have their request for withdrawal of funds blocked until they have repaid their credit cards and other loans made by the bank in full. Only then will the funds in the deposit account be released. From the bank's point of view, this may seem a sensible move. However, for those customers who urgently have need of funds saved for emergencies, such as health issues, this can cause considerable delays, inconvenience and added stress.

I recently heard from one couple that had to return to the UK urgently because of illness. They had a mortgage and a credit card with their Spanish bank and their payments were fully up to date; indeed, they had been responsible and model customers of the bank for many years. Unfortunately, they also maintained all of their savings, which were not insignificant, with the same bank. However, when they attempted to withdraw some of their funds, their request was rejected. After visiting the bank and discussing their problem, they were told that their deposits were held as security and that they would have to repay all of their mortgage loan and their credit card before their savings could be released. When I met the couple concerned, they were distraught and appeared to be 'trapped' in a situation whereby they could not afford to return to the UK, as they no longer had readily available funds.

This is not the first time that I have heard similar stories, although this was the one with the most serious implications for the couple concerned. Most expats that I have spoken to are unaware of the current linkage between bank deposits and credit cards, and I suspect that this is a change in the 'terms and conditions' that have been applied during the banking crisis. All banks operate slightly differently and it may be wise to check the current situation with your own bank.

The moral of this story is clear. If you are fortunate enough to have funds deposited with a Spanish bank, make sure it is not with the same bank where you have a mortgage, credit card or a personal loan. Experts also suggest that it is wise to maintain a percentage of your funds in the UK - just in case. As the old adage says, 'Don't put all your eggs in one Spanish basket'.

'The Barcelona Problem'

This problem began when we moved into our new home in the Canary Islands. It was a new build property, and like most new builds it came as a shell, meaning that there was no fitted kitchen, shower, bathroom or any of the modern fixtures that I initially expected to see. Unlike new properties in the UK, ours and similar properties were sold with this feature as a "consumer advantage", on the basis that fittings are a matter of consumer choice and the size of one's pocket. However, I suspect this "consumer advantage" is more of a culture of laziness on the part of builders than anything that is consumer orientated. Even after being lulled into a false sense of security by a smooth talking estate agent, I did feel that leaving bare wires hanging from walls and ceilings in order to "give us a choice of light fittings" was taking "consumer choice" a little too far.

Finally, after much discussion with several kitchen fitters, we decided upon a colour scheme and units for our new kitchen. Sadly, it was now August; in other words, the 'Silly Season' had begun, which meant an almost total closedown of offices, shops and services for, in theory, two weeks in August. However, in reality, this means that few things, including the temperature, get back to normal until late September or even October. The very nice sales lady then raised the issue of appliances for our new fitted kitchen.

We would have preferred to take our time in selecting the all important appliances from local electrical stores, but as we were shortly due to move into our new home, we took the very nice sales lady's advice that "if you don't order now, you won't get much before Christmas". She noticed that my eyebrows had shot heavenwards at that point, and she quickly added, "You see, everything has to come by boat to the island from Barcelona. Barcelona is the problem, not us."

I was not convinced; we had already come across 'the Barcelona problem' many times before. It was, and still is, a comment freely trotted out by any salesperson that doesn't have what we want in stock. Be it kitchen appliances, parts for the car, packets of tofu or even jars of Marmite. I become weary each time 'the Barcelona problem' is mentioned.

My partner and I glanced at each other and nodded. Yes, although it would be more expensive, it would clearly be to our advantage to order the kitchen appliances right away, and to have them fitted at the same time as the kitchen units. We had already decided upon the type and brand of appliances that we would like, but each time we asked for a specific brand, the very nice sales lady smiled and shook her head. "No, I am sorry. If we order this, it will take at least six weeks. It is 'the Barcelona problem', you see."

"What about Fagor, Hoover, Hotpoint, Bosch, Whirlpool?" I went through most of the brands that we knew of, or at least had some experience of. The very nice sales lady shook her head sadly, making the same point, "I'm so sorry, we don't have these in stock. If you order these, they won't be here until Christmas. We have the Christmas break, New Year holidays and King's Day; it could be well into next year before they are fitted. It's 'the Barcelona problem', you see."

Being sensitive to our disappointment, the very nice sales lady opened the drawer of her desk and with a flourish pulled out a fat catalogue from a French brand that we knew very little of, but I won't mention the name here. Looking back, I don't think we had even heard of the brand before. The appliances looked good, and they were in the stainless steel finish that we wanted, and the very nice sales lady assured us that all of the items that we required were in stock. Anyway, surely a washing machine is a washing machine, irrespective of brand?

We ordered a fridge freezer, cooker hob and oven, dishwasher, washing machine and microwave, and all would be installed the following week. "You won't be disappointed," the very nice sales lady assured us as I handed over my credit card. "They are all reliable machines and will last for years."

When the very nice sales lady had mentioned "for years", I hadn't realised that she had really meant "for four years". In reality, each appliance has lasted just over four years. Each appliance has died in the last few months and, today, the last appliance, an electric oven, blew up after four years and two days from purchase. I am now convinced that all the appliances that we had purchased came installed with a pre-determined obsolescence time clock.

What have I learned from this experience? Firstly, I now twitch at very mention of 'Barcelona', and will avoid visiting the city for a while and, secondly, I will buy German-made appliances in future.

"Double the Difference"

The recent furore about the checkout lady in a UK supermarket, who refused to serve a customer whilst she was chatting on her mobile phone, rightly brought many people to the defence of the good lady. After all, she was doing a valuable job, but being treated as a 'nobody'. Sadly, her employers were not as aware of basic good manners, and awarded the wayward customer with a voucher and apologised for the incident, when they should have promoted the checkout lady to supervisor. However, sometimes the reverse situation occurs, in Spain and the Canary Islands, as well as in the UK.

More often than not, I am faced with a checkout operator who is chatting to the person on the next till, chatting on the telephone, or to the next customer. In the Canary Islands, this is complete with lots of hugs and kisses, which takes even more time. Now, I know that plans for the weekend, the latest boyfriend/girlfriend and the wellbeing of the new baby are vitally important, but preferably not at the expense of mistakes on my shopping bill. Indeed, the UK checkout lady's situation is often reversed here, and it is I who is made to feel like a 'nobody'.

As a result, I often refuse to place items on the checkout belt until I am sure of receiving the checkout person's full and undivided attention. They often look surprised as I glare at them and refuse to co-operate, but I explain with a smile and they usually see my point of view. Old fashioned? Maybe, but I am now old enough to recognise that basic good manners are rather important in any society, and I rarely give way on such issues nowadays.

How many of us check our supermarket till receipts? We all should, of course, but the reality is often that we are so pleased to escape the supermarket checkout that many of us don't bother. Mums coping with kids screaming for sweets, an ice cream or the latest Xbox game usually wish for a rapid exit from the supermarket till. We tend to rush on to the next task and assume that Carlos or Maria has got it right. Until recently, I rarely bothered either. This was mainly due to my laziness in recognising a carrot or a courgette on my till receipt, as I can never remember the correct names in Spanish. It really is just too much like hard work to worry about on a hot day.

We tend to use one particular supermarket, because it is within an air-conditioned commercial centre, and also includes many other stores that we like. The fruit and vegetables are also particularly good, and with most of the produce coming from the islands rather than being flown in from the Spanish Peninsular. However, I have felt on several occasions that the overall total was higher than calculated, and resolved to make a closer check in future.

The first time that I checked the receipt, it appeared that we were charged for an additional packet of coffee that we did not have. The check out girl shrugged and sent us to customer services. After a long wait we were refunded both with the cost of the coffee plus the same amount again as an apology. This, we were told, was part of the store's "Double the Difference" guarantee to shoppers if mistakes were made. I accept that mistakes happen, and I was both grateful and surprised at the generosity of the offer, as well as the sincerity of the apology.

Over the following weeks, we checked our till receipts carefully and with the exception of one visit, an error was revealed each time. The errors usually were related to a single item being scanned twice. Once, there was an error in our favour, where the item had not been scanned at all, which we duly reported. I am confident than none of the errors were due to a deliberate policy of ripping off the customer, but a mixture of incompetence and untrained staff.

This week, I checked once again to find that two bags of carrots had been charged when we had only bought one. I went to customer services to request a refund, which was given to me promptly and without fuss. However, this time, there was no offer of "Double the Difference", which was surprising given the previous visits. I asked the customer services lady why this was, and the reply was brief and to the point.

"There have been so many claims and the company is losing more money than it can afford and so they stopped it," was the response.

I know that I am only a customer, but might it be cheaper to train staff properly and to supervise them more effectively to avoid errors in the first place?

Meanwhile, do check your till receipts carefully in the future.

The Memory Tree

I guess that most of us have our own special Christmas traditions, which follow the same routines and rituals each year; either on our own or remembering the traditions of years gone by. For me, it is putting up the Christmas Tree on 6 December, which is the day that the Christmas season really seems to step up a gear in the Canary Islands. Needless to say, getting a real tree is neither economic nor environmentally desirable in the almost treeless landscape where we live, and so we have to make do with an artificial one.

We call our Christmas Tree, a Memory Tree, for that is really what it is. As we decorate our tree with ornaments and garlands, we remember the many people that have contributed to it over the years. It has become one of our special traditions and one that many of our friends have contributed to over the years. Maybe it is a glass bauble, a knitted toy or something special given to me by some of the children that I taught long ago. We also have small decorations collected from some of the countries and cities that my partner, David, and I have visited over the years. "Ah, yes, that blue china bear was from an Amsterdam market", or maybe "Do you remember the trams in San Francisco?" are some of the predictable, yet strangely comforting, conversations, that David and I have with each other every year, as we recall the special memories associated with each trinket or toy that we are about to hang.

We hang decorations that once adorned the trees in our grandparents' homes, or in the homes where we grew up. Some decorations have a special poignancy for us, such as the brightly coloured knitted robin that David's mother so skilfully made for us many years ago, and who passed away this year. We hang the small, brightly coloured, rainbow flag on our tree and remember the tiny charity shop in the Castro district of San Francisco where we bought it. It was during our visit many years ago after the city had been decimated by the AIDS virus, and at a time when it seemed that there was very little hope for HIV sufferers.

At last it was time for the crowning glory of our Memory Tree, the Christmas Fairy, which was to be placed at the top of the tree. I take it gently from its box and blow off the dust. Although it now looks a little worse for wear, the fairy is still fit for another year. My Auntie Mim gave it to me for my first Christmas, and I have always treasured it.

As I hang it on the tree, supported by the usual lump of Blutack and Sellotape, I remember a little girl whom I taught in my very first year as a teacher. I had been to great pains to plan a lesson that retold the Christmas story, as well as preparing the appropriate visual aids for the religious education lesson. The children sat in awe as I told them the story of the first Christmas, and the visit of the angel to Mary to tell her that she was expecting a baby. The children sat in silence and later went back to their desks to write their account of the story, whilst being reminded that as it was end of term and parents evening was a few days later, I wanted to show off their best handwriting.

Silence reigned in the classroom for a good twenty minutes, before Michelle arrived at my desk and proudly presented her work. In her very best handwriting, she had painstakingly written "Mary and the Fairy" at the top of the page. Well, I couldn't really argue with this. After all, as I was growing up, people kept telling me it was an angel and not a fairy at the top of the Christmas tree, which I guess was all about religious correctness. I always protested; after all, have you ever seen an angel carrying a wand? Anyway, we all need a fairy at Christmas.

Surviving Christmas and the New Year – Top tips for expats

It is December 21st, and the world is supposed to end later today. If you are reading this, well done; we have survived another global catastrophe. If not, I guess it means that we didn't. Alternatively, we may have all slipped into another universe, in which case, I hope the journey was a pleasant one and that you went up rather than down, if you see what I mean.

So, how did the Christmas and New Year festivities go? I hope they were full of booze, tinsel, joy and laughter, but not necessarily in that order. If the partying didn't go quite as planned, maybe you have missed something obvious and would like to consider some of my suggestions for next year.

• Did you remember to buy Christmas cards when you last visited the UK? You know that the oldies cannot cope with email cards, yet they don't want one in Spanish or French either. It's no good sending one of last years Marks and Spencer's boxed selection, because although you think the oldies have lost their marbles, they do remember that kind of detail.

• Did you commit the unforgivable sin of sending one of those jolly, animated fluffy dog and cat email cards that were so popular five years ago? Yes, I also sent them until a few years ago, and I'm still receiving therapy. I finally realised that most people cannot be bothered to open them, and those that do, get bored with listening to 'The Twelve Days of Christmas' over and over again. Just a tip, classy cards are now regarded as cool! (and preferably those with lots of glitter)

- Still on the subject of Christmas cards, did you send self-righteous emails telling everyone that you will not posting Christmas cards this year and that you will be sending the money to a water well charity in Africa? Forget it, you have fooled no one. We all know that you forgot to send the money to the charity, even though you possibly meant it at the time.

- Never send the dreaded 'Everything is lovely' Christmas newsletter to all your friends and relatives. They will just hate you for it. They really don't want to know that you are spending a sun and gin filled existence in the Costas, or that your daughter has married a banker in the South of France. Human nature being what it is, they would probably be much happier to read that you have lost your job, become an alcoholic or made bankrupt. Sad, but true.

- Have you received less cards, letters and gifts that you sent out? People may have moved house, died without telling you or are so jealous that you have escaped to the sun without them, that they no longer want to know you. Get over it.

- How did you respond to callers over the festive period? When they asked you, "How are you?" Did you tell them the truth? Did you tell them that you were about to have a beach barbecue on Christmas Day? If you did, they will probably hate you for it, because they spent Christmas trying to get to Aunt Dorothy's through two metres of water, because their home was flooded. Unless it is your mother, or a handful of very special friends, most callers couldn't care less how you are or how you spent Christmas. Surprising, but true.

• Now to the thorny issue of presents. What did you send the grandchildren for Christmas? Maybe you took the easy way out by sending a cheque. Sadly, you may have finally realised that the kids never get the cheque anyway because their mother uses it for a pre Christmas night out with her latest boyfriend. Maybe you did the wise thing and sent them tasteful gifts, courtesy of Amazon? However, do you really think that fourteen-year-old Naomi will still appreciate a pink Barbie doll, or that Giles is still interested in playing with the latest baby-faced Action Man? Then again, maybe he does. Don't be surprised if the 'thank you letter' never arrives, and always keep the receipt.

• Did you give your husband, wife or partner a thoughtful present for Christmas? No, I don't mean something that they needed, but something that they wanted? One acquaintance gave his wife a hedge trimmer for Christmas a few years ago. She was not impressed and used this incident as grounds for divorce the following year. So be warned.

• Did you cherish your friends over Christmas? The old expression that friends are the family that we create for ourselves is so true. Many of us fall into the trap of thinking that we have many friends. In reality, of course, most are acquaintances and we only have a handful of true friends, so look after them and make them feel special.

• Did you remember to make or order mince pies before Christmas? It is an almost unforgivable sin to invite Brit expats to your home for a 'social experience' and not to offer them a mince pie. On a more serious note, do remember that many of your friends may be recovering alcoholics anyway, so always check that the mince pies do not include brandy in the recipe, however small the quantity.

• When did you take down the Christmas decorations? This is a dilemma for many Brits living in Spain. Remember that the Christmas celebrations only get into full flow on the 5th and 6th January in Spain, because it is King's Day. Taking decorations down before this special day is a gross insult to your Spanish friends and neighbours, yet all Brits know that leaving decorations up after 6 January is bad luck. Personally, I lurk in the patio before midnight on 6 January, removing the decorations and lights before midnight, when most of the locals are so merry that they no longer care anyway. It is called cultural sensitivity.

• Did you make any New Year resolutions, and proudly told your friends all about your latest diet or that you have finally kicked the weed habit? Don't do it, they will just regard you as sad. If you must have a New Years resolution, keep it to yourself. You won't stick to it past the second week of January anyway.

Finally, was it all worth it? Probably not, but do try a little harder next year. The best treat of all is that we have managed to reach 2013. May I wish you all a Healthy, Happy, Sun-filled and Marmite eating New Year!

Expat Considerations for the New Year

Have you made any resolutions for the New Year? I know many expats who have made a number of very determined resolutions, and I applaud their efforts in doing so. However, I do get bored with hearing about "My Diet for the New Year", "Going to the Gym, "Learning a New Language" and all the rest. How many of these will be kept, I wonder? Worst still, resolutions have a nasty habit of making us feel even more demoralised than before they were made. Personally, I like things to be a little more flexible.

I no longer 'do' resolutions, but instead I have 'considerations', which are basically areas for personal improvement that I can consider doing, forget or modify as I go along. Is it a cop out? Well, maybe, but we shall see later. Here are just a few recommended 'considerations' to think about, which are based on a number of e-mails that I have received from 'Twitter' readers last year.

Don't try to create a mini Britland in the Costas

One of the greatest frustrations for expats is failure to convert the Spanish to becoming British. They are quite happy as they are and, indeed, this is one of the reasons why you moved in the first place. Watch, listen and delight in being welcomed into a new country. Remember, the days of Empire are long gone.

Try not to be too cynical about politicians

Don't fall into the trap of believing that all politicians, local councillors and people in power in your new country are corrupt and don't know what they are doing. Granted, some are, but many are ordinary people trying to do their best, and often in difficult circumstances. If in doubt, do consider the Leveson Enquiry, the UK Parliament Expenses Scandal, Jimmy Savile, Libor rate fixing, naughty banks, Hillsborough... The UK is by no means perfect, and 'people in glasshouses...'

Don't blame the Euro

Come off it, you have had it good for too long with the strong pound and weak euro. All good things come to an end. Believe it or not, the euro and the Eurozone are here to stay, and I foresee that the euro will eventually become a stronger currency than the pound. (Letters of complaint to the European Central Bank please)

Don't complain about the EU

Like it or not, the EU is here to stay. Sadly, it is that troublesome island off France that is causing the problems, not the EU. Maybe the EU is better off without the UK? (Letters of complaint to the UK Prime Minister please)

Don't read the Daily Mail

Don't read the Daily Mail, which has recently been rebranded to the Daily Hate, if you wish to remain sane or do not wish to gain a distorted view of the world. If you have been reading it regularly for more than three months, it is probably far too late to fully recover, but you could consider rehab or a course of treatment with a good and patient psychologist. Needless to say, teachers, civil servants, bankers and public sector workers should never go near a copy.

Don't moan about the fall in property prices

The point of buying a property is to live in it, and not to sell it at a vastly increased price. Maybe you paid more for it than it is worth now. The bottom line is that you are very fortunate if you own a home of your own. If you wanted a secure investment maybe you should have stuck to Premium Bonds. Get over it and just enjoy living in it.

Don't moan about the lack of your favourite products

Now, I know as much as the next man about Marmite shortages and the rest. Adopt new tastes or adopt a cunning plan, such as inviting generous guests to stay on condition that they bring suitcases of goodies for you.

Don't fly the UK flag too often

It is not a great idea to hoist the Union Flag on your apartment roof too often. Locals may get the wrong idea. Just imagine if the Pakistan flag was flown outside your house in Mansfield? Sorry, maybe it was...

Don't complain about the TV programmes

We all know that foreign television is mostly reality TV and game shows. Get yourselves a satellite dish or find a crafty way of accessing the BBC on-line instead. Before long you too will be pleading to pay your UK TV licence fee.

Don't complain about the food

Sorry, but chicken and chips and pie and chips may not be readily available. Try paella and chips instead.

Don't shoot the messenger! Some of these 'don'ts' may be a little harsh, but are true for many. Lets start the New Year on a positive note, but if you cannot, well, maybe it really is time to go home (wherever that may be).

A Healthy, Happy and Peaceful New Year to Expats everywhere!

Ten Years On

It is ten years to the day since my partner, David, and I set out on our big adventure for a new life in Spain. After many years of working within the UK education service, it was time to move on and begin a new life in the sun. As much as we had both enjoyed our work in schools, work-related stress had taken its toll on David's health in particular, and we both realised that the UK was no longer where we wanted to be.

I guess the worst part of getting ready for our move was telling our family and friends. Most of our family were very supportive, realising that it was a good opportunity for us, although I do remember one elderly aunt wailing in horror when she heard the news. Close friends helped and encouraged us, whilst a few not so close friends completely ignored us once they heard the news that we were about to escape the evils of the UK climate. Yes, we learned a great deal about envy and jealousy too, which both hurt and surprised us.

The big day finally came; our Bournemouth home was now empty and in the hands of the estate agent, our possessions sold, given away, or collected by Pickfords for shipping to the Costa Blanca. Barney, our much loved and self-willed corgi, had been collected and taken for a long holiday with David's brother; he would join us a few weeks later. We drove in silence to Southampton airport, both wondering if we were doing the right thing. That evening, before the flight, we stayed in a nearby hotel, where two good friends joined us for the evening and treated us to a kind of 'farewell dinner'. It was a good evening and we shall never forget their kind words as they left us at the airport the following morning.

After long flight delays at Southampton Airport, we were told, ironically for us, that as it was very hot weather, the aircraft would need more fuel in order to leave the short runway at Southampton Airport to fly to Alicante. It all seemed a very lame excuse at the time, but we found ourselves flying back to Bournemouth where the plane would take on more fuel and finally head towards our destination. We would be much later arriving in Alicante that originally planned, but as we had visited our new home in the Costa Blanca a few weeks earlier, all we needed to do was to drive to our new home and fall into bed.

Nowadays, I often use the expression that "All is never as it seems in Spain", and I guess that this was our first taste of what was to come. We arrived at our new home to find that the water and electricity had been disconnected. We had no torches or candles and the light was rapidly failing. We could see that our neighbour's home was lit and so they clearly had electricity; it seemed to be a good time to introduce ourselves to them. They smiled when they heard of our plight. These were not smiles of cruel amusement, but friendly recognition of what had happened to them, and others, just a few months earlier. We were told that these things happen in Spain, and that we would have to check with the builders the following day and ask for a "builders supply". Little did I know of this particular scam at the time, but it turned out to be yet another way by which more euros could be extracted out of the unsuspecting expat moving to the Costa Blanca.

Meanwhile, our new neighbours were kind, friendly and helpful. They offered to feed us and put us up in their spare room for a few nights. Little did we know at the time that this was to be the beginning of a long and valued friendship, as well as a glimpse of the supportive self-help network that many generous minded expats share with other expats in trouble. As the days of waiting for a permanent electricity and water supply to be installed turned into weeks, there were many occasions when we were grateful for our neighbour's hosepipe thrown across our joint wall so that we could have a shower, or a hot meal cooked for us.

Ten years on, I am often asked if I would do the same thing again. The answer is most certainly, yes. We have had many adventures, mostly good times and a few bad times in Spain, but overall the country has been welcoming and a positive experience for us. We have also learned a great deal; for example, recognition that the Brit way of doing things is not always the best way, and to be open minded and sensitive to other cultures and other ways of doing things.

I guess that I have also learned to be more patient. Both David and I tend to be people who like things done yesterday. We tend to be impatient when tasks are completed slowly or inefficiently, or we have to wait a long time for things to happen. This is, of course, one of the first lessons that the newly arrived expat learns when arriving in Spain. Things tend not to happen quickly or at all. Impatience, being aggressive or short tempered to people in authority simply makes matters worse, yet a smile, a few words of encouragement, or a box of chocolates often works wonders.

Laws, rules and regulations also tend to change with the wind. What was acceptable or legal yesterday may not be legal or acceptable today. Local officials also tend to have their own very flexible interpretation of the law, which can be frustrating, but not worth getting into a sweat about. This is not to say that we take matters that are wrong lying down. There are certainly areas where a complaint or a protest is required and is effective if handled correctly. As our knowledge of the Spanish language and culture has improved, so has our ability to communicate, challenge and complain effectively, if required.

I am also often asked if I would do things differently if I had the opportunity. I guess I wish that I had taken the learning of languages more seriously when I was at school. French was the only option on offer for most of my time at school, which I disliked intensely. Learning Russian in the sixth form was a different matter. As a rebellious teenager, I had chosen Russian mainly to annoy my parents, yet I liked it and was quite good at it. Learning Spanish much earlier in life would have made our lives in Spain so much easier, and I despair of those expats who refuse to even make an attempt.

Will we ever move back to the UK? I have also learned never to say never. Spain and the Canary Islands are now our home and during our occasional visits to the UK we now feel that it is a foreign country. Life and circumstances change and we never know what is in store for us. None of us know what old age, infirmity and loneliness may bring, and what our decisions or available options will be at that time. Meanwhile, from where are now, I know that we have made the right decision and fully intend to continue to enjoy our home and life in the sun.

2699868R00116

Printed in Germany
by Amazon Distribution
GmbH, Leipzig